2787

HEROIN
USERS

To the memory of Paul Band

The bloody pubs are bloody dull
The bloody clubs are bloody full . . .
The bloody pies are bloody old
The bloody chips are bloody cold
The bloody beer is bloody flat
The bloody flats have bloody rats . . .
The colour scheme is bloody brown
Evidently Chickentown

(John Cooper Clarke, 1980)

THE NEW HEROIN USERS

Geoffrey Pearson

Basil Blackwell

Copyright © Geoffrey Pearson 1987

First published 1987

Basil Blackwell Ltd
108 Cowley Road, Oxford, OX4 1JF, UK

Basil Blackwell Inc.
432 Park Avenue South, Suite 1503
New York, NY 10016, USA

British Library Cataloguing in Publication Data

Pearson, Geoffrey
The new heroin users.
1. Heroin habit – England, Northern
I. Title
362.2'93'0922   HV5822.H4
ISBN 0–631–15396–9
ISBN 0–631–15621–6 Pbk

Library of Congress Cataloging in Publication Data

Pearson, Geoffrey.
The new heroin users.
Bibliography: p.
1. Heroin habit – Great Britain.
2. Narcotic addicts – Great Britain.
I. Title.
HV5822. H4P425   1987   362.2'93'0941   87–5157
ISBN 0–631–15396–9
ISBN 0–631–15621–6 (pbk.)

'Evidently Chickentown' by John Cooper Clarke
© 1980 SBK Songs. Used by permission.

Typeset in 10 on 12 pt Palatino
by Columns of Reading
Printed in Great Britain by
Billing and Sons Ltd, Worcester

Contents

Preface

An enormous amount of public attention has been given to Britain's new heroin problem which, according to a recent parliamentary committee, is 'the most serious peace time threat to our national well-being' (Home Affairs Committee, 1985). There can be no doubt that this is a serious problem in our midst which could become much worse if we do not act promptly and decisively to contain it. But what is the new heroin problem really about? Is it a largely a question of evil gangsters plotting the downfall of the younger generation? Or is it a problem that has been encouraged by the self-indulgences of wealthy pop stars? Does it afflict people from all walks of life, or is it a problem confined to certain sections of the population such as the young unemployed? Why do people get involved with heroin in the first place, when its notoriety is so well known and publicized? Is heroin a drug habit that is impossible to relinquish? Indeed, does it lead inevitably to death?

This book attempts to allow heroin users to speak for themselves, about how they first encountered heroin, what they think about its effects on their lives, and then how they have tried with different measures of success to 'come off' and 'stay off' heroin. All the people whom you will meet in this book are perfectly ordinary young men and women whose lives have nevertheless been altered and often damaged by their encounters with heroin. And, other than their involvement with heroin, they share something else in common: which is that they live in some of the most deprived parts of the north of England, which is one of the areas where the new heroin problem has become most serious.

Short sections of this book have appeared previously in a report to the Health Education Council, published by Gower, which examines in more detail some aspects of service delivery and agency co-operation in drug liaison initiatives. Here, I have kept professional and technical considerations such as these to a minimum. Even so, a small point of detail needs to be mentioned which concerns language and how people who use drugs such as heroin compulsively should be described. In professional circles the words 'addict' and 'addiction' are nowadays often frowned upon. At first, they were replaced by terms such as 'drug dependency' or 'drug abuse'; later 'drug misuse' came to be preferred, together with the expression 'problem drug user' instead of 'addict'. It will be found that I have often stuck to the words 'addict' and 'addiction', however, for the simple reason that these are the words which addicts themselves most often use, and this, when all is said and done, is their story.

A second question of language concerns speech dialects. This research was carried out in the north of England, and one of the many inequalities to afflict the north is that their speech is often regarded as somehow inferior and even unintelligible to people in the south of England. A significant aspect of this inequality is that the reverse is not true: northerners are perfectly capable of understanding the slang and dialect of London and other parts of the south, as well as what George Orwell once described as the 'plummy voice from the radio' which now also dominates television broadcasts. In trying to allow heroin users to speak for themselves, then, it seemed wrong to pretend that people from the north of England always speak with 'received pronunciation' or 'standard English', so that wherever possible I have stayed as closely as I could to what people actually say and how they actually say it. This means that some of the people who figure in this book speak quite archaic forms of standard English. For 'you' and 'yours', for example, they will sometimes say 'thee', 'thou' and 'thine'. For 'yourself' they sometimes say 'thissen' or 'yersen'; for 'herself' they sometimes say 'hersen'. Someone from 'south of Watford' may think that this is either terribly quaint, or even the speech of a verbal incompetent. But it is not. If, in some parts of the north of England, you are met with the greeting 'How's tha doing then?' (meaning 'How are you doing then?') it would be wrong to think that you have just encountered someone who is either a caveman or an idiot. If, on the other hand, you sometimes think that it sounds a little like Chaucer, you are perhaps nearer the mark: some aspects of northern dialects carry the imprints of much older forms of 'standard' English.

Another difficulty of dialect concerns the patterns of sound which are sometimes produced. In the phrase, 'in the house', for example, 'the' will often be shortened to 't'. This is then sometimes rendered 'in t'house', although this is not helpful for people unfamiliar with Northern speech because it can give the impression that people are making a sound pattern something like 'in ta house'. This, as I recollect it, is how a generation of actors and actresses tried unconvincingly to reproduce northern dialects during the British 'realist' cinema of the 1950s and early 1960s. I will use a different convention in order to render this speech in a written form. Where 'the' is shortened to 't', then for ' . . . in the house', I suggest that ' . . . in't house' captures the actual flow of someone's speech more effectively. 'She's off't heroin now', then means 'She is off the heroin now'. 'But tha's been off't smack now for six month' means 'But you've been off the smack now for six months'. And so on.

I cannot claim to be an expert in the technical aspects of dialect speech, but I grew up in Lancashire and my ear for the language suggests that this is a better way to capture the flow and vigour of some aspects of the northern dialects. However, as far as Liverpudlian speech, or 'scouse', is concerned I simply lost my nerve. I do not have sufficient familiarity with those forms of speech – whereby 'work' becomes 'werk', 'girl' becomes 'gairl', and 'got to' becomes not just 'gotta' but 'gorra' – to feel confident that I could faithfully reproduce them.

In writing this book I have accumulated a large number of

debts. First and foremost, to Shirley McIver and Mark Gilman who worked with me gathering together the interview material on which the book is based, and whose energy, commitment and insight simply cannot be repaid. Next, my thanks go to the Health Education Council who funded this research, and particularly to Peter Linthwaite, Deborah Leonard and Deryck Lambert who were always helpful and supportive. The fieldwork was carried out while I was still employed at the University of Bradford where I held a Readership in the School of Applied Social Studies, and there my colleagues gave me every kind of assistance, especially Susan Noble who was the secretary to the project. Since then I have moved my job, and discovered a new intellectual companionship among my colleagues in the School of Social Work and the Centre for Criminology at Middlesex Polytechnic. Nigel South and Nick Dorn from the Institute for the Study of Drug Dependence taught me a great deal, as well as being good friends, and I also benefited enormously from conversations with Roger Lewis from SCODA, the Standing Conference on Drug Abuse. In the early days, before the project was even underway, I received welcome encouragement from Mary Tuck at the Home Office Research and Planning Unit, and also from Jason Ditton at the University of Glasgow whose friendship and intellectual stimulation have been simply invaluable. Peter Barham, as always, was there to urge me on when things became difficult. Throughout everything, Marilyn Lawrence helped me to stick with it even when I felt that I no longer knew what I thought about the new heroin problem, which was quite often. Finally, there are the heroin users themselves whose voices are heard in this book and whose contribution cannot be acknowledged directly, but must remain cloaked in a variety of disguises and pseudonyms. They invariably admitted that they had made a bad mistake when they became involved with heroin. But any mistakes in the book itself are mine.

Geoffrey Pearson
London

A Heroin Epidemic?

. . . and the next minute it was everywhere, like. It just sort of took Liverpool by storm. (Jack, 22 years, Merseyside)

We saw it spread . . . spreading all around't town through every area . . . it were like a black cloud weren't it, just kind of seeping over here. (Brian, mid-20s, South Yorkshire)

And then all of a sudden, everyone you met like . . . Everyone was on it . . . It was hardly ever heard of was it? It's really been in the last two years, something like that . . . (Sharon, 21 years, Merseyside)

The heroin problem which has emerged in Britain in the course of the 1980s is an essentially novel phenomenon. Whereas North American cities such as Chicago and New York experienced their initial heroin epidemics nearly forty years ago in the late 1940s and early 1950s, Britain has been something of a late developer. Heroin use had been almost completely unknown here until the late 1960s, when a brief surge in the official statistics caused significant amounts of alarm. Even then, the official number of heroin addicts was no more than 3,000 and the problem was largely confined to London. During the 1970s the official figures registered a

1

gradual increase, but nothing more. Then, somewhere between 1979 and 1981, awful rumours began to emerge of a new heroin problem involving new words and phrases to describe it – 'chasing the dragon', for example, and 'skag' – a problem which was showing itself most prominently in some of the more run-down areas of our towns and cities.

At first, many people seemed prepared to discount these rumours as merely another 'moral panic' in the more sensationalist newspapers. But the rumours proved to be well-founded. Heroin had started to become more easily available in cheap and plentiful supply, working its way along new trade routes from the opium poppy fields of Iran, Pakistan and the North West Frontier. The new heroin users were also quite different from the older generation of vaguely bohemian 'junkies', in that they were more likely to be recruited from otherwise quite conventional working class neighbourhoods. Another vital difference was that whereas the older 'junkie' users had invariably injected heroin, the new heroin users were more likely to smoke the drug by heating it on aluminium foil and inhaling the fumes – now known variously as 'chasing', 'dragoning' or 'having a toot'.

The practice of smoking heroin had been long established in many parts of the world – including Hong Kong, from where the expression 'chasing the dragon', known in the Chinese Cantonese dialect as *Júi Lùng*, had been taken – where it no doubt derived from traditional customs of opium smoking, although just how it came to be recognized in Britain that heroin could be smoked and did not need to be injected is one of the mysteries of the new heroin problem. But it was a recognition that proved to be crucial, in that it removed a formidable cultural barrier against self-injection, which undoubtedly allowed the heroin habit to spread more widely than would otherwise have been possible. This is not to say that people no longer use heroin by means of intravenous injection – 'fixing', 'hitting it up', 'cranking' and so on. People do still inject heroin, sometimes having started with 'chasing'. Even so, injection is now probably a minority pursuit, although the preferred means by which people use heroin is itself subject to widespread local and regional variation. An added complication is that the imported 'brown' heroin from the new sources in south-west Asia had been prepared for smoking rather than injecting. In order to be rendered soluble for injection purposes, 'brown' heroin must first be acidified – with lemon juice, for example, or a drop of vinegar. All this, and more, is now common knowledge in the world of the new heroin users.

By the mid-1980s, the official number of heroin addicts had increased alarmingly by British standards to more than 12,000. It is a fair guess that the actual number of heroin users in Britain by this time was well in excess of 50,000, and possibly somewhere between 60,000 and 80,000. It needs to be said, however, that this was still only a tiny problem in comparison with some other parts of the world. In the USA, for example, the number of narcotics addicts probably exceeds half a million, with maybe as many as 7,000 heroin addicts in the ghetto districts of east and central Harlem in New York alone, and roughly 27,000 people registered on the methadone programme in the whole of New York City. In Hong Kong, with a total population of only four and a half million people over the age of eleven years, 7,000 people report daily on the government's methadone programme and there are no fewer than 37,000 officially registered heroin addicts who tend once again to be most densely located in the poorest neighbourhoods. Of course, these figures – although huge by British standards – only indicate what is known and counted. The unknown size of Hong Kong's heroin problem is perhaps best described as simply unknown, although on some estimates it might embrace upwards of 100,000 people, many of whom nowadays inject heroin as well as smoking it.

Even if we accept the more gloomy estimates of the actual size of Britain's new heroin problem, suggesting that there might be as many as 80,000 users, this does not even remotely approach the scale of heroin misuse elsewhere. If this were evenly spread throughout the British Isles, it would be no more than a thin smear of a problem. But it is not evenly spread. Rather, the new heroin problem is still a highly scattered and localized phenomenon which affects some towns and cities more seriously than others. Even within a town or city with a major problem, it will tend to be concentrated in certain neighbourhoods and virtually unknown in others. Moreover, where the problem has tended to gather together in dense pockets within our towns and cities, this will usually be within neighbourhoods which are the worse affected by unemployment and wretched housing. This is not to deny that heroin can visit people of all social classes and backgrounds – as the headlined excesses of wealthy pop stars and Oxford undergraduates testify. But where the new heroin problem is most serious it will be found huddled together with the most serious poverty of unemployed Britain.

The headlines do not lie, then, although they can sometimes mislead. There has been too much of an emphasis in the press, perhaps, on pop celebrities who have succumbed to heroin. Also, it would be wrong to think that very young people in their early teens are the most common recruits to the new heroin problem: very young users are not unknown, but they are exceptionally rare and the new heroin users are more likely to be young men and women in their late teens and early twenties. But having said all that, one should not disguise the fact that where the problem bites hardest it is a truly sad and awful social difficulty. Indeed, in those working class neighbourhoods where the new heroin problem has assumed an epidemic form in recent years, it is so bad that the headline writers of Fleet Street simply would not have the literary command to describe how bad it is.

Nor can statistics even begin to encompass the awfulness of the problem in Britain today. It is better approached as something which seeps into people's lives, friendships and families. And rather than talking over the heads of the people whom this problem affects, as we so often do in policy debates of various descriptions, it seems better to allow the new heroin users to speak for themselves in order that we might learn something from their experience. What they then have to say, when given this opportunity, does not always conform to the common stereotypes of heroin addiction. These stereotypes will often describe the problem as originating with 'evil pushers' who set out to trap helpless victims in the snares of heroin misuse, whereas heroin users themselves tell a different story – of a problem that begins among friends. The stereotypes of heroin will also depict someone's involvement with the drug as nothing more than a horrible chemical enslavement which it is impossible to throw off, whereas heroin users' own accounts are better understood as those of people exercising choices and decisions in their lives – even though they will often come to regret those same choices and decisions. Heroin is also understood as an instant and immediately addictive substance, although what heroin users describe is something more insidious which creeps into their lives by stealth, slowly and imperceptibly. And finally, the stereotype portrays heroin as inevitably a 'killer drug', the 'white death'. But dramatic pronouncements about death seem hardly relevant to what the experience of the new heroin users most typically amounts to. Rather, it is an experience of being terribly alive, caught up in a drab and stressful treadmill, waking up each day to the gnawing preoccupation with where the next £5 'bag' of heroin will come from. It is a question not of dying, but of living by one's wits from day to day amidst some of the worst poverty that has been inflicted on unemployed Britain in recent years. Then, the grim acknowledgement of what is happening within their lives as friendship falls apart.

The highly self-dramatized accounts of the personal trials of those who move within the social orbit of wealthy pop stars and debutantes might encourage the belief that heroin addiction amounts to nothing but indulgence and excess. But if we listen carefully to the experiences of the new heroin users, theirs is a destiny born out of something quite different.

I
Friends not Pushers

I was just gave some, for nothing like, by a mate . . . I liked the feeling . . . I just got into it that way. (Colin, 23 years, Manchester)

My boyfriend's friends were all using it and that, and giving it to me . . . They were always offering me chases, and at first I was refusing it, but then I gradually slipped into it. (Josephine, 28 years, Humberside)

I was curious so I tried it and I liked it . . . There was a few of us, we were all good mates and that like, we all tried it and eventually everyone just got hooked. I've said to you before, it's no one's to blame. It's you. You're the one that's saying, 'Yeh!' . . . (Eddie, 21 years, Merseyside)

At the School Gates:
the Initial Offer

The first time that someone is offered heroin it will be by a friend. Or maybe by a brother or a sister. But always by someone well known, liked and even loved.

Of course, the most widely publicized image of how someone first encounters heroin is quite different. It depicts a 'pusher' driving down to the school gates in a flash car and handing out free samples of 'sweeties' in order to get children hooked. In the spring of 1984, when the news of Britain's new heroin problem first began to break, there were even allegations from one part of the country that heroin had been injected into school milk and spinkled on to school dinners. These allegations were, quite rightly, immediately rejected by people with sound local knowledge, including not only educational officials but also a leading representative of a parents' group in the area who said, 'I have never heard of anything like this happening. Things are bad enough here, but not that bad' (Guardian, 2 May 1984).

Even so, these sensational images refuse to go away, perhaps because they help to reinforce the view that people who become involved with heroin are passive victims of a wicked conspiracy which sets out to trap them unwittingly into addiction. It is a view which heroin users themselves will sometimes promote, as if they shared no responsibility for the choices which they made when they first said 'yes' to an offer of heroin, and each time they said 'yes' until they were indeed 'hooked'.

It is no doubt true that there are people driving around in expensive motor cars who live off the proceeds of the heroin trade. But they do not venture down to the school gates, or anywhere near them. Nor do they deal in 'free samples', or even in £5 'bags' or 'wraps' which are the lowest form of exchange within the heroin economy. The massive profits which one hears so much about in connection with heroin are to be found not at street level, but in the commanding heights of the heroin economy among major traffickers who deal only in bulk transactions involving kilogram and multi-kilo quantities of heroin (with a value something in excess of £20,000 per kilo at current prices). And anyone who has that kind of money to lay out, and that kind of stake in the heroin trade, not only has better things to do than knock out £5 bags of heroin adulterated with glucose and brick-dust, and containing only milligram quantities of the drug itself. They are also not going to take stupid risks, such as dealing to schoolchildren. Indeed, people with that kind of stake in the heroin economy probably never even see the drug, but simply put up the money which brings heroin into the country. Theirs is not an unimportant role in the heroin traffick, but it is not through them that people will first encounter the drug.

The stereotype image of the 'pusher' trapping people into addiction is not only wrong, it is also unhelpful. First, it denies that people have any choice in the matter of whether they become involved with heroin. So that if one is trying to encourage people to exercise different choices – to say 'no' in other words – it offers no insight into the contexts in which these choices will actually have to be made. The danger of the misleading stereotype of the 'pusher' is that it warns people against something that is never likely to happen. Equally, it leaves them unprepared for what will actually happen when, and if, they are offered heroin. If people are to be encouraged to say 'no' to heroin, or any other kind of drug for that matter, then they must first be told what it is that they will be saying 'no' to: it will not be to the wiles of a 'pusher', but to the gift of a friend. Indeed, it is a sobering fact that if the stereotype of the 'pusher' were true, and that initiation into the world of heroin did come through the blandishments of strangers rather than friends, then the numbers attracted to the habit, which can spread like wildfire through a neighbourhood friendship network, would be considerably reduced.

Friends of friends: 'I was curious so I tried it'

The role of friendship in helping to spread the heroin habit cannot be over-emphasized. Whenever heroin users are asked how they first came across the drug, they give one version or another of the same story:

'How did you get into it yourself then?'

'Just through my mates really, going to their houses, and well one of my mates, he'd say "D'you want a chase?" or whatever, and I just started getting into it like that . . . and the next minute it was everywhere, like. It just sort of took Liverpool by storm.' (Jack, 22 years, Merseyside)

Or:

'I was just gave some, for nothing like, by a mate. And the feeling is different, I liked the feeling . . . and after that I started buying my own bags, £5 bags and that, I just got into it that way.' (Colin, 23 years, Manchester)

Sometimes people remember that they tried heroin on the very first occasion that they came across it:

'I was at a party with some friends, good friends that I'd known for ages. And there was some heroin going round. I'd heard about it, but I'd never actually seen it before. And, they were smoking it on foil . . . you know, chasing it. This friend who'd brought it with her said did I want to try? There was no pressure on me, or anything like that. They were obviously enjoying it, so I thought "Why not?" That was the first time.' (Julie, 29 years, West Yorkshire)

For others the experience was different. They had at first been reluctant to try heroin, but in the reassurance of the company of friends they had eventually decided that it was acceptable:

'My boyfriend's friends were all using it and that, and giving
it to me . . . They were always offering me chases, and at
first I was refusing it, but then I gradually slipped into it.'
(Josephine, 28 years, Humberside)

There is no hint of any element of compulsion in these offers of
heroin within a friendship network. It is simply that someone
who has already tried the drug wishes to share what they have
found to be an enjoyable experience with other friends, even
though it might be an experience which they live to regret:

'Like, a few people I knew had tried it, and said it was good
gear. So I tried it . . . I thought it was the best, like, that I'd
ever tried . . . Sorry I did like.' (Joey, 20 years, Merseyside)

Getting involved in heroin might, on the other hand, reflect
a more active ambition on someone's part. As one young man
remembered it, when heroin had first appeared in his locality
he had been attracted by what he saw as a lifestyle involving
risk and excitement with which he wished to be associated:

'When the heroin first came round, there was a few into
it . . . just a few . . . and they were, you know, the elite.
And I just wanted to get into that, like.' (Michael, 21 years,
Merseyside)

Sometimes, although not often, it was the first serious
involvement with an illicit drug that a person had ever had:

'It was the first drug I ever took.'
    'Really?'
    'I've never . . . I have smoked a draw, like, when I've been
there and people have passed me it. I've had a drag because
it was there. But I've never actually gone out and bought a
draw or anything like that . . . it never really bothered
me . . . that was the first thing.'
    'And was that with friends?'
    'Yeh, with some mates who were already on it, you know,
and they said, "Here y'are, do you want a chase?" and all
that like.' (Paul, 24 years, Merseyside)

But more commonly, people had already experimented with

other illicit drugs, such as cannabis ('draw', 'blow' or 'dope' as it is known) or amphetamine sulphate ('speed' or 'whizz') before they tried heroin:

'It's like everything else, the heroin came round and . . . I was curious so I tried it and I liked it . . . There was a few of us, we were all good mates and that like, we all tried it and eventually everyone just got hooked.' (Eddie, 21 years, Merseyside)

Or it might be not so much curiosity about a new drug, but that within a circle of friends who had already established a pattern of illicit drug use, heroin was first used as a substitute if the drugs which they normally used were not available for some reason:

'You see up till then we'd been having, started having a bit of sulphate before then, didn't we? . . . And then a friend come round, said I couldn't get nowt sulphate, so . . . got this heroin, and that was it.' (Linda, mid-20s, South Yorkshire)

But whichever way it was phrased, these heroin users remembered the drug as something which circulated among friends, and which quickly became a widespread habit within their neighbourhood:

'And a lad we knew says to us, "Do you want some smack?" . . . and me and a friend had a bag between us . . . And then all of a sudden, everyone you met like . . . everyone was on it.' (Sharon, 21 years, Merseyside)

Free samples and child victims:
'Kids are still kids around here'

It is clear from these heroin users' recollections of how they first met the drug that the stereotype of the 'pusher' does not conform to their experiences. What, then, of other aspects of the stereotype such as the 'free sample' to get someone hooked, or the stranger lurking at the school gates?

It is as well to say at the outset that a single dose of heroin, whether as a free sample or not, does not get someone 'hooked' on the drug: it is necessary to take heroin on a regualr basis for some time before someone becomes dependent on it. This immediately suggests that there is something phoney about the idea of getting people hooked by 'free samples'. You would have to have an awful lot of heroin to throw around (and therefore an awful lot of time and money to invest) in order to contemplate trying to get people 'hooked' by such a method. It is simply not the way that the heroin economy works.

Invariably, when asked whether children and young people of school age were involved in the local heroin scene, users and ex-users issued a blunt denial. As for the question of 'free samples', this was sometimes simply held up to ridicule. For example:

'Like I said, I've been around the smack scene a long time. Not just here but all over the place, and I've never come across any of these free samples you hear about . . . Chance'd be a fine thing! And as for the young ones, well . . . they haven't got the money have they? Where are they gonna get the money from to buy smack, regular like? You hear all this stuff in the papers. That fourteen-year-old lad in Liverpool what died, that kind of thing. It's sad, alright. It's sad. But they're giving the wrong impression, as if it was all the young ones. I've known . . . I don't know . . . maybe one or two fifteen- or sixteen-year-olds at it. I've heard of that down in London. But it's the exception. It really is, believe me.' (Gary, 27 years, Humberside)

Even so, the rumours about very young heroin users persist. They do not seem to be merely fabrications put about in the more sensational news headlines, for they also enjoy a widespread popular appeal, whether or not this conflicts with a more detailed knowledge of local circumstances.

'To be honest with you, I've heard there are, but I've never seen hardly nothing . . .'
'You hear a lot about it though, don't you?'
'I've heard that it's up at that school and all that . . . but

my little brother, I mean my little cousin who goes there, he
says it's not . . . No, I think there isn't.'
   'Why's that? Won't people sell it to kids, or what?'
   'Yeh. No one will sell it to kids. No one. I've never known
a lad under the age of 16 to be on it. Never. That's straight-
up, that . . . although . . . Yeh, that's the truth, I haven't.
But em, there's a few on cannabis and all that, younger kids,
but that's harmless. I've never known a kid to go on smack,
never . . . ' (Joey, 20 years, Merseyside)

How then do such rumours enter into circulation? One
possible reason is that heroin users themselves will sometimes
claim to have started on the drug at an earlier age than they
actually did in order to attract some status to themselves, by
way of notoriety:

   'No, everyone round here who's at it, they're all over
   eighteen, in their twenties, older than that too. There just
   isn't no kids on it, and that's that. Alright, some of these on
   it now, they'll tell you they started on it when they were
   thirteen and all that. But they didn't. It's all talk. They think
   they get status, that kind of thing, you know. If someone
   says, "I started on it when I were twelve, thirteen", that kind
   of thing . . . they never even *saw* it, know what I mean, until
   they were . . . oh I don't know, much older than that. In any
   case, no one'd sell it to them, either, even if they wanted it.'
   'Why not?'
   'Why not? Because it's just wrong . . . out of order . . .
   you know.' (Kevin, 23 years, Manchester)

And this brings us up against another problem with the
myth of very young people being snared into addiction by
unscrupulous 'pushers', which is that heroin users and
ex-users will often express strong feelings against supplying
drugs or offering drugs to young people:

   'Oh, they wouldn't sell it to kids . . . phhh . . . no way like,
   it's just out of the question. I've never, ever actually seen
   young kids buying it.' (Eddie, 21 years, Merseyside)

As one young man described it, the prohibitions against
supplying heroin to younger people might sometimes touch on

wider loyalties of family and kinship, which for him also
extended towards a gut-feeling that was opposed to certain
kinds of crime (but not others) being used in order to support a
heroin habit:

'If people stood dealing outside the school gates, I reckon
they'd get battered for it. Their big brothers'd come up and
everything. I reckon I'd punch someone myself, like, selling
outside the gates. I would. Giving it to kids, like, it's only
gonna mean one thing isn't it? Old women getting mugged
and all that . . . Cos little kids, like, they're too scared to do
some things [i.e. shoplifting and housebreaking] but they'd
mug an old woman and all that like, cos it's easy. That's why
I wouldn't like the kids to get on it.'
'Is there much violence involved?'
'No, not really, not that way like . . . I knew one lad that
mugged a woman. He got battered everywhere . . . a real
outcast, like. No one'd sell him smack or nothing.' (John, 19
years, Merseyside)

It is not that heroin users are a band of guardian angels. Far
from it. John himself had embarked upon an almost reckless
criminal career in order to sustain his heroin habit. Nevertheless, there is a kind of morality operating here which acts
against the likelihood that heroin would become easily
available to young people. As another young man put it, there
were 'rules and do's and dont's' within the world of heroin:

'You hear a lot about people selling it at school gates. Do
you find that ever?'
'No, I don't think that's true. It never happens round
here . . . There is, like, sort of rules to it. You know what I
mean, like, sort of rules to getting involved in the whole
smack scene. You don't sell it to kids. And you don't like
even give any to a kid . . . people have got, there's still a bit
of self-respect involved . . . It's not completely out of hand.
There's sort of, like, rules and do's and dont's sort of thing.'
(Jack, 22 years, Merseyside)

The likelihood that any kind of morality is to be found in the
lower reaches of the heroin economy is invariably discounted

in the sensational news stories about the 'evil pushers'. It exists, nevertheless, also extending to the commonly held view among heroin users that it is wrong for people who do not use heroin themselves to supply it. Having initially encountered heroin in the company of friends, as someone's involvement with the drug deepens, they first begin to make the acquaintance of small-time user-dealers from whom they buy their £5 bags and wraps and then become vaguely aware of the outlines of a hierarchy of deals and transactions – from £5 and £10 bags, through weighed half-grams and grams, to quarter-ounce, half-ounce and ounce deals – although only very few heroin users will ever get close to the people who deal in ounces, given that the going rate for an ounce of heroin is in the region of £1,000. One way of describing these gradations is to distinguish between those people who deal in heroin only for monetary gain, known contemptuously as the 'bread-heads', and those who do it for the 'smack' in order to supply their own habits, the 'smackheads'. Within the 'folk wisdom' of ordinary heroin users it is held to be somehow morally improper for people to deal in heroin only for the money, thus making for strange, but little understood tensions between different levels of the heroin economy.

What also needs to be said is that a certain amount of caution must be exercised when dealing in heroin, not only in the commanding heights of the heroin economy where fortunes can be made and lost, but also at the lowest levels. Someone wishing to buy heroin, even from a small user-dealer, will need either to be a familiar face around the 'smack' scene, or to have an introduction from a user who is already known and trusted. There are too many risks involved in selling to strangers, so that although local dealers are often known and described as 'pushers', they do not actually 'push' heroin in the sense of using aggressive sales techniques in order to attract new customers. Rather, they wait for people to come to them. And what all this adds up to is that at the 'street level' of dealing – which is where it really counts in terms of the dissemination of heroin within a neighbourhood – very young people or strangers are unlikely to be able to get their hands on heroin, even where it is widely available:

Cheryl   I'm one o't youngest round here. There's no young uns . . . And like, I've got to say this like, all't pushers who I know, I've gotta give this to 'em, they won't push it on people . . .

Wendy   You've gotta go for it . . .

Cheryl   Yeh, you've gotta go for it yersen.

Wendy   They don't go looking for people . . .

Cheryl   They don't, do they? No.

Question   You hear about people selling outside the school gates. Do you ever come across that?

Cheryl   No, there's none o' that . . . None o' that, is there?

Wendy   What?

Cheryl   Waiting outside school gates.

Wendy   . . . [incredulously] . . . No . . .

Cheryl   It's not like that. Kids are still kids, aren't they, round here?

Wayne   I think when people talk about, like, young uns getting into it . . . you know, people getting kids into it and kids getting into it, I think it's just as important like older people who're into it and all. It's . . . you know what I mean . . . like you've gotta take as much notice o't old uns as what you have young uns. Cos it's just, that's problem . . . heroin. It's not your age or owt. It's just heroin itsen . . . that's problem, isn't it?

(Cheryl, Wayne and Wendy, early 20s, South Yorkshire)

This is a significant observation, because the preoccupation with very young heroin users can easily distract us from where the real problem lies. And it is not among schoolchildren, nor as a result of 'free samples' handed out by strangers, but among young people in their late teens and early twenties. This is guaranteed in part by the way in which heroin circulates, at the point of initiation, within friendship networks. It is also a consequence both of the risks involved in dealing outside well known circles of acquaintances, and of the moral prohibitions which exist within the heroin subculture against involving very young people.

Of course, although very young heroin users might be a

rarity, they are not entirely unknown. If I am right in describing one barrier against their involvement with heroin as a 'morality' within the drug scene, then in common with other systems of morality it can sometimes break down. Eddie from Merseyside, for example, who had 'never, ever actually seen young kids buying it' and who considered that selling it to them was 'out of the question', did nevertheless know that they sometimes got it from somewhere:

> ' . . . but like, I've been walking along the street and, like, *girls* of fourteen have said to me, "Have you got a drop of vinegar on you lad?" I mean for hitting it up in the arm . . . it makes you sick.' (Eddie, 21 years, Merseyside)

Had he, then, ever come across 'free samples' which were intended to lure you into addiction?

> 'I've known people who are really into it, you know, who've been blasting a gram a day and things like that, and . . . you know, the dealers get to know them, good customers and that like. If you're doing that, you can get it laid on and pay later if your face is well known. But you've still gotta give 'em the money. Cos, if you don't . . . that's it, like, fucking hell . . . people'll be after yer, know what I mean?'
>
> 'But what about all this you hear, about people giving out free samples to get you addicted?'
>
> 'No, I know nothin' about that . . .'
>
> 'You always have to pay for it?'
>
> 'Oh, I've had toots off people I've known, you know . . . Like it's . . . like I've said to you before, no one's to blame.'

Eddie, in fact, had an unusually direct sense of where the responsibility for his involvement with heroin lay. He did not blame 'free samples'. He did not blame 'pushers'. He had got into it, he said, with his friends: 'We were all good mates and that like'. But nor did he blame his friends:

> 'There's no one to blame for it. It's yourself. You're the one who decides to get into it, so it's on your plate. It was no one's fault. I just got into it. It was sheer, "Oh that's nice like, I'll get into that" like . . . I've said to you before, it's no

one's to blame. It's you. You're the one that's saying, Yeh. If yer can say no, well fair enough, you're laughing aren't ya? If you can't say no, it's just hard shit. I'm not blaming anyone for my addiction, it's my own fault like. I accept that.'

First Steps:
the Early Experience

If a person has been offered heroin and accepts it, what happens next? What are the likely outcomes of this initial experience, and what does the drug actually do for people in these early stages of use? This might seem an obvious question; but, as it turns out, it is not at all an easy question to answer. At first, heroin seems to affect different people in very different ways, so that for some it is immediately enjoyable, while for others it is something of a mixed blessing – or is even thoroughly unpleasant. And even for those who do like the effects, what they like about them can vary enormously.

Not nice: 'It made me so ill'

How someone responds to heroin will depend to some extent on what other kinds of drugs they have used, with which heroin might then be contrasted favourably or unfavourably. Because it is certainly not always the case that the drug will initially be experienced as pleasurable. It is not uncommon, for example, for opiates to make people feel terribly sick when they first use them, which can itself be a sufficient deterrent to further experimentation. But this initial sickness cannot be relied upon to deter people. Indeed, many people will persist in taking heroin in spite of the fact that it makes them feel unwell.

Jack, for example, had tried most other drugs that had been available to him from time to time – cannabis, amphetamines, LSD – although he had at first been reluctant to try heroin when it was offered to him and had refused offers from friends for nearly two years before he did eventually try it. He was just past his twentieth birthday when he first got into it with some friends, and he immediately enjoyed the drug even though it sometimes made him feel sick:

'After a couple of times, like, if I had too much at once then you might be sick. But even after you're sick, well, you feel even better like after you've been sick. You know what I mean? Like if you're having it and you start being sick, you think "Oh no, I feel sick" and you go and be sick . . . and feel even better then. So being sick didn't really put you off.' (Jack, 22 years, Merseyside)

A heroin user in the Manchester area pointed to one acquaintance who was nearly always sick and who was in fact regarded locally as a bit of a joke:

'Look at that lad Derek, he's been using for years on and off and he's still sick as a dog. Goes upstairs to the bog, even before he has a toot, so he's ready like . . . Y'know ready to spew up so he doesn't get it all down his trouser legs . . . It never put 'im off it, and there's others like that.' (Alan, 24 years, Manchester)

Two young women from South Yorkshire in their early twenties, discussing their drug experiences in the company of the brother of one of them, agreed:

Wendy When you first have it, like, you don't like it do you at first?

Cheryl No, it makes you sick . . . ugh . . . I were spewing up all't time . . .

Wendy But you always keep trying again don't you, and . . .

Cheryl I did.

Wendy You know it's wrong to take, and you know you don't like taking it, but . . . you know, you keep trying again.

Wayne   It's influences off other people I think . . . You know, other people are doing it, so . . .

(Cheryl, Wayne and Wendy, early 20s, South Yorkshire)

Josephine, an older women in her late twenties from another part of Yorkshire, had the same story to tell:

'And then when I did use it, how I got a habit I don't know, because for months it made me so ill . . . I just kept taking it.'

'But why?'

'I don't know, I just can't understand it myself. I suppose it was because it was there . . .' (Josephine, 28 years, Humberside)

Different people react differently to heroin, however, as a young man from Liverpool explained:

'Did it ever make you sick?'

'No, that's one thing I've never, ever done. Well, to be honest, I've been sick about only . . . I can count it on one hand, about five times, something like that, that's all. I don't know why. My mates used to spew up in front of me, and I used to laugh at them . . . One of 'em said that I wasn't, you know . . . like they'd chase it and they used to hold it in, cos they'd only buy like £5's worth, where I was blasting like £25's worth . . . Like they'd hold it in for about as long as they can, till they're blue in the face and blow it out . . . I used to just hold it in for about twenty seconds . . . just swallow it and just blow it out. They used to think it was because I didn't hold it in long enough. But I done it one night . . . I held it in as long as all of them. Still never spewed up. I was sick the other week though, that was two weeks ago. I think what makes you sick is if you drink water. That's what makes me sick, if you drink something and that . . . Whenever you spew up like, whenever I've been sick, it's always brought me down off it . . . Mm, like, say you're sitting 'ere wrecked, enjoying it y'know, and then you spew up, you're not wrecked then. So like I'm glad I don't spew up, like . . . Ugh, they go white and all that, and then they say, "Oh I'm being sick" and all that . . . I'm glad I'm not like that.' (John, 19 years, Merseyside)

And a similar version was given by another young man from the same area:

> 'It doesn't hardly make me . . . I don't sort of vomit, you know what I mean. Like, even when I've had loads, I can't be sick on it . . . Sometimes I have, you know when I've had loads of tea and loads of drink . . . that's what makes you sick . . . urghh . . . ' (Gavin, 22 years, Merseyside)

At first sight, it might seem puzzling that people will persist with something which makes them feel ill. But it is not really surprising in view of the fact that initial encounters with other drugs (including those that are socially sanctioned, alcohol and tobacco) often make people feel ill until they learn how to take the drug properly and how to handle its effects and interpret them as enjoyable. The first surreptitious 'drag' or 'swallow' on a cigarette, with its attendant effects of dizziness or nausea, lays a sound foundation upon which people will persist with drugs which are not immediately or obviously pleasurable. So, too, the 'never again' feeling which invariably accompanies the first hang-over, or the sickness which follows from excessive drinking, are powerful lessons that these inhibitions must be overcome if an intoxicant is to be enjoyed. In this respect there is no reason why heroin should be different from other drugs.

Really nice: 'You feel just great!'

If the likelihood that heroin will make someone feel ill cannot be relied upon to deter the user, then what are the pleasurable effects which override these unpleasant sensations? People who have used heroin will agree that it is a drug which produces a wonderfully pleasant experience of well-being. But if we try to define this experience a little more precisely, it proves to be surprisingly difficult. It is a common observation that drug users employ a very loose vocabulary to describe and label the internal states which they experience. Words such as 'stoned', 'high', 'buzz', 'wrecked' (which all refer to pleasurable effects) not only sum up the limits of this restricted vocabulary, but are also employed to describe the effects of a variety of different drugs (cannabis, amphetamines, opiates) which are otherwise totally dissimilar. This limited vocabulary nevertheless seems quite sufficient to describe and identify the experiences brought about by illicit drug use, for it has suffered little if any alteration in the past fifteen years. Drug users will also sometimes report that certain drugs (cannabis and amphetamines) can give them 'paranoid' feelings, or that they feel out of touch with events and 'spaced out'. Being 'spaced out', however, is not necessarily a bad thing to be. Finally, as far as heroin is concerned, when it is injected the immediate impact is known as a 'rush', and whether smoked or injected the state of temporary euphoria which can be produced is known either as 'nodding off', 'gouching' or being 'gouched out'.

Why the drug culture has not generated a more complex vocabulary to describe the effects of drugs is unclear, and contrasts sharply with the rich variety of words used to describe the drugs themselves. Amphetamines, for example, are usually known as 'speed' or 'sulphate', although it is increasingly common for speed to be called 'whizz'. Heroin itself is usually known as 'smack', or 'skag' in some areas, with less common expressions in parts of Britain such as 'henry' or 'nanoo'. Cannabis, of course, has attracted almost a whole dictionary of descriptions, including the now largely defunct 'pot' and other obsolete terms such as 'shit' or 'charge', together with the more common expressions such as 'dope', 'ganja', 'grass', 'weed', 'blow' and 'draw', and so on. 'Blow' and 'draw' seem to be particular favourites at the moment, although this terminology is subject to immense local variation and changes in fashion. But as far as the effects of drugs are concerned – 'stoned', 'high', 'wrecked', 'buzz' – there is surprisingly little change or variation in patterns of verbal usage within this highly restricted vocabulary. So that a typical description of the initial effects of heroin will often be set in a characteristic vagueness:

> 'First, when I was on it, like, I donnow . . . it made me feel dead pleasant, I donnow, dead . . . as if I never had a care in the world, d'you know what I mean? It wasn't like a

"high" . . . You know exactly what you're doing and all that. It was just, like . . . you haven't got a care, y'know, it was just different.' (Paul, 24 years, Merseyside)

Sometimes, heroin's effects are described in straightforward and immediate terms, as simply pleasurable:

'It's just the *nicest* drug going, you feel just *great!* Just . . . phoo . . . blows our mind, like, you start nodding and . . .' (Eddie, 21 years, Merseyside)

'I thought it was the best, like, that I'd ever tried . . . Sorry I did, like . . . [laughs] . . . It was just different completely, just better . . . ' (Joey, 20 years, Merseyside)

Other people thought of heroin as something which brought on a sense of peaceful relaxation:

'With smoking, it comes on you gradually . . . and you just feel dead relaxed and dead tired and what have you . . . ' (Mick, 23 years, Manchester)

Still others experienced the initial effects as immediate, bringing with them an urgent feeling of great personal strength and power:

'As soon as you chase it, it just hits you straight away . . . and you just feel like *the boss*, like . . . ' (Jack, 22 years, Merseyside)

And, to further complicate matters, there were those who liked not only what they experienced as heroin's immediacy, but also the helpless feeling of being 'wrecked' and 'gouching':

'So what's so special about heroin then?'
'The way you take it. I loved it, like. I know it sounds, it's horrible when you look at it . . . You know, but when you're just doing it, like . . . Saves you building up and all that [i.e. when heroin is smoked on foil, it is less trouble than preparing a cannabis joint] . . . you know, making it. And the hit's brilliant, when you first start. Like, you sit there . . . and it's just like, helpless. You must look bad and all that, cos I've seen my mates and thought they did . . . But like,

I'm just sitting there gouching . . . it's brilliant.' (John, 19 years, Merseyside)

Or again:

'Like when I first took it, I remember the first I had, it just blew my mind . . . and like, it wasn't just a little toot I had, it was a fucking load. You know what I mean, it just really done me in. And like, I liked that, you know what I mean . . . I liked it too much.' (Gavin, 22 years, Merseyside)

For others, it was enough to rely upon the tried and trusted vocabulary of the drug culture:

'Me and a friend had a bag between us. Well, we only had half the bag and we were wrecked . . . really stoned . . . your first one, like it's just too much, you're just like walking on air.' (Sharon, 21 years, Merseyside)

'I liked the buzz I got.' (Wendy, 21 years, South Yorkshire)

'It was just . . . whoosh . . . an instant hit, you know, like the best high ever . . . ' (Barry, 22 years, Manchester)

Mixed feelings: 'You just don't care about nothing'

The initial effects of heroin, then, are experienced quite differently by different people. But if the active elements of heroin's effects are open to a wide variety of forms of description and interpretation, these people were nevertheless in agreement that they liked the drug's effects. And another common feature in many of these accounts was the drug's capacity to take away a person's worries:

'The actual time I went on it, I'd just finished with my girl and come back down here. And as I say, I got in with my old mates who were on it . . . and I suppose I was on a bit of a downer myself like, a bit depressed and all that. And as I say I took some heroin, and all my worries that I had just seemed to float away, you know what I mean. Like at the time, when I broke up with my girl, I suppose I could've come home for a week and then gone back and fixed it all up. But it wasn't like that . . . I come home. I got into the gear. And it just happened so quick . . . before I knew it I wasn't thinking about my girl or the baby . . . I just wasn't. When I had heroin, I didn't have a problem. I didn't have any worries.' (Paul, 24 years, Merseyside)

An odd feature of Paul's account was that what he first found attractive about heroin, namely that it took away his worries, later came to be experienced as its major handicap:

'You just become dead to the world . . . it's just a totally different experience, you know what I mean. You're more or less a walking zombie. Got no interests. You've got no feelings for anyone . . . and I mean anyone.'

But this ambivalence should not surprise us, because Paul was trying hard to stay off heroin and to patch his life together again. So that while he could remember the initially pleasurable effects which had released him from the worries he felt were crowding in on him, he was also very keenly aware of the wretched effect heroin had subsequently had upon his life.

The same conflicts show through in other people's experience. For example:

'At first, it was just great. Me and my mates . . . we didn't care about nothin', you know having a good time, having a toot and that. But then, it sort of turned round . . . you just have a smoke, smoke the gear, and that's it like. There's nothin' else to bother about. I stopped going to football . . . and I used to love football, you know, the match. I stopped going to concerts, going out like. That was it . . . ' (Billy, 22 years, Manchester)

Eddie, who earlier had described heroin as 'just the nicest drug going', later described how it came to mean something else as it affected his group of friends:

'We all just went dead weird to one another . . . "Fuck you", like . . . We weren't interested. I lost interest in my family, my girl and everything like . . . ' (Eddie, 21 years, Merseyside)

John who had previously thought that the helpless feeling of being 'wrecked' was 'brilliant' also came to see it differently:

'You just don't care about nothing . . . the way I treated my mam, like, I mean that's as low as you can get. I just didn't care. You just don't know what you're doing like.' (John, 19 years, Merseyside)

This ambivalence is present in so many accounts which people give of heroin's effects, and it alerts us to a major difficulty in piecing together an adequate version of people's experience of the early stages of their drug involvement. Trying to describe how people first come into contact with heroin and their early experiences with it is necessarily a process of reconstruction from the memories of heroin users and ex-users who have been using it for some time. Direct accounts of early experiences with heroin are much more difficult to come by because experimental users and people in the 'first flush' of heroin use are notoriously elusive – to researchers, treatment agencies or health educators. Why they should be so elusive is not difficult to understand. For them heroin use is a new adventure which, although it will often imply a high degree of risk (not only because of the illegality of heroin, but more significantly its very notoriety), will not have become a problem in a person's life. The problems only come later, and it is only when these various problems arrive – whether with family or friends, or with the police and the courts – that there is a likelihood that someone will either step out into the public domain and 'declare' their involvement with heroin, or be 'caught in the act'. Before that, in the early stages of use, the heroin user keeps his or her activities as a secret within a small cluster of friends and fellow users.

The necessary process of reconstruction of a person's early encounters with heroin from the recollections of more experienced users carries with it certain hazards. It is not that heroin users are unreliable informants, or unresponsive to questioning. On the contrary, people who have got into difficulties with heroin are often only too happy to talk about their problems, and will sometimes say that they hope that their experiences might act as a discouragement to others who might otherwise be tempted to take the same risks. Indeed, this co-operative attitude is precisely where the problems of reconstruction begin: the ex-user will often feel under some obligation to offer a cautionary tale-of-woe, which sifts out the more pleasurable and exciting aspects of drug use, and thereby falsifies what is at issue when people first start to use heroin.

At the extreme, we are given highly self-dramatized accounts by ex-addicts which place undue stress on the miseries and enslavements of heroin use – the 'monkey on your back' and 'cold turkey' – at the expense of the pleasures which they initially undoubtedly experienced. And although this emphasis on the eventual miseries of heroin use is perfectly understand-able when someone feels that their life has been wrecked by the drug, it nevertheless fails to account for why people should use heroin in the first place. So that when listening to the cautionary tales of ex-addicts, it is always necessary to guard against giving them an unduly privileged status – as if, coming as they do from direct experience, they represent fully authenticated accounts that 'tell it like it really is'. Rather, we should listen to the complex shifts of emotion and emphasis in their recollections, which reflect not some kind of unreliability or lack of truthfulness, but the real ebb and flow of a damaging but nevertheless pleasurable relationship to the drug.

The negative emphasis which is so often encountered in the recollections of heroin users is also encouraged by the attitudes of the friends and families of ex-users, who will distrust and sometimes discourage the expression of any lingering positive feelings towards heroin or those who use it, fearing these as a sign of potential relapse. A similar mechanism was seen to be at work in James Beckford's (1985) research on the experiences of ex-Moonies who were often encouraged to suppress one side of their ambivalent feelings towards their former life. It was perfectly alright for ex-Moonies to give vent to their hostile feelings about their experiences, but not to indulge in recollections which implied residual loyalties to the past or to former friends. A guarded watchfulness characterizes the family relations and friendships of former heroin users, sometimes leading to a tetchiness in people's dealings with each other, as when the ex-user feels that the family is being maybe too watchful:

Cheryl Mother! As if I'm going to go back onto smack now
         anyway . . .
Mother I've never said you are.
Cheryl No, but the way you said that just then . . .

                         (Cheryl, 20 years, South Yorkshire)

In these kinds of circumstances, it can sometimes be difficult
to get heroin users and ex-users to talk about both sides of
their ambivalent relationship to the drug, so as to reflect both
the positive as well as negative aspects of their drug
involvement. It is easier sometimes for people to stick to the
well-trodden moral agenda which renounces heroin as nothing
more than a horrible enslavement. We have already seen how
Cheryl and her friend Wendy, for example, found that at first
heroin made them sick. But they kept using it nevertheless.
Why? When they were encouraged to talk about what they
found pleasurable about heroin use, in the company of
Cheryl's mother and her brother, although they were eventually able to share their feelings and explore some of these
difficult aspects of the ex-user's ambivalence, this was not
always easy. When this area was first touched upon, for
example, for one brief moment a window was opened on the
attractions of heroin, only to be quickly closed again:

Question So what is it about heroin, compared to blow or
          speed or . . .
Wendy   Y'know, heroin. It teks everything away, don't it?
Cheryl   Oh aye. No worries.
Wendy   You feel reet at ease, like . . . don't you, your
          mind's reet . . .
Mother   You were reet at ease when . . . [inaudible,
          everyone shouting at once] . . . becomes one big
          worry though, don't it!
Wayne   Teks all yer worries away and then becomes a
          bigger one itsen
Mother   Yeh, it does.

This kind of tension must be part of the daily life of many
families who are trying to adjust to the problems caused by a
member's heroin use. If Beckford's (1985) work on the
experiences of ex-Moonies can be used as a basis of compari-

son, then these tensions will often require the ex-user to deny
one side of their ambivalent feelings towards their past life.
There are significant differences, of course, although Beckford's discussion of the difficulties faced by the 'apostate' who
has quit the Moonie faith and returned to his or her family are
highly reminiscent of the siftings and reconstructions of the
past lives of heroin users who have relinquished heroin. Ex-
Moonies were often reluctant to discredit or disown entirely
the movement which had previously supplied them with
comradeship and spiritual support. Their families, however,
did not want to hear about these residual feelings, afraid that
they might indicate a potential 'relapse'. The strategy sometimes adopted by the ex-Moonie, then, was to refuse to discuss
their former links with the movement at all – although silence
itself could be interpreted by their families as indicating the
feared possibility of backsliding.

Tangled webs of family emotion such as these also help to
shape the ambivalence and sometimes conflicting accounts
which ex-users give of their former lives, leading often to a
straightforward denial of any pleasurable aspects of drug use at
all. Denial is not, however, the most helpful basis on which to
come to terms with complex experiences and emotions. Nor is
it necessarily the most effective way to dissuade other people
from getting involved with heroin – especially when health
education advice based on such partial, one-sided accounts of
the heroin experience is offered to those who might already
have begun to experiment with the drug, or who have friends
who have tried it. In which case, they will know from their
own experience that heroin can be extremely pleasurable: they
might therefore conclude that those who deny the pleasures of
heroin simply do not know what they are talking about.

No feelings: ' . . . it puts you, like, in Ethiopia at first'

The early experiences of heroin use are subject to a wide
variation. The drug often makes people sick at first, although
this does not mean that they will go no further in their
experimentation with heroin. For some people, however, it is

an instant 'buzz' and a 'hit'. For others, heroin's attraction is
that it brings with it relaxation. For some it offers an enhanced
sense of personal power. For others it means being 'wiped out'
and 'wrecked'. The majority of heroin users will already have
had a wide experience of other drugs before they tried heroin.
For some, however, it will have been the first drug that they
had really tried, other than alcohol and tobacco. But with
different shades of emphasis, one common feature was the
ambivalence felt towards the drug, while another was that
heroin 'took your worries away' and made people feel 'at ease'
with themselves and in their minds.

On occasion, this feeling of release from external pressures
and worries was so all-pervasive in a person's recollections of
their early heroin use that the positive drug-effects (in the
sense of a 'buzz' or a 'hit') hardly seemed to play a significant
part in their attachment to the drug. For them, heroin was a
'solution' to other life problems which beset them: low income
and family poverty, wretched housing and unemployment.

For example, Linda and Brian are a married couple in their
mid-twenties who both developed heroin habits a few years
ago. Unlike many of the new heroin users, they had injected
the drug almost from the start, having previously been
accustomed to injecting amphetamine sulphate on an occasional, recreational basis which had been an established aspect
of the drug culture in the part of Yorkshire in which they lived.
Their initial encounter with heroin, as it transpired, was almost
accidental in that they had not sought it out. Indeed, heroin
hardly played any part at all in their version of events, except
as something which had enabled them to forget about their
other, quite considerable worries. So that, when asked to
describe their initial experience with the drug, they chose to
answer in a roundabout way in which other concerns were
much more to the forefront of their attention:

Question How did you get into heroin, then?
Linda   Oh, it were terrible
Brian   We lived in't front room . . . like it's knocked
         down now'
Question Oh, you weren't living here?

Linda	No, another house.
Brian	They knocked it down it were that bad. We ended up wi' . . . there were no gas, there were no watter, we had to go next door for us watter . . .
Linda	Chimney fell down . . .
Brian	Chimney fell in't back, and they wouldn't let us use gas fire, they wouldn't let us use it. So we got no gas, no electricity, nowt . . . And we were living in theer, and they were still wanting us to pay rent for it, wouldn't get us out or nowt.
Question	Who was that, the council?
Brian	Yeh. And we lost a young un through it like . . . Linda were pregnant and she lost a young through it. After that . . . that's what did it weren't it, that's what started us?
Linda	Yes.
Brian	Too many problems and, like, we had some henry one day like, and we went back to't house, and we forgot all about house, because we were . . . you know . . . just didn't see nowt, so it were . . .
Linda	You see up till then we'd been having, started having a bit of sulphate before then, didn't we?
Brian	Yeh.
Linda	And then a friend come round, said 'I couldn't get nowt', sulphate, so . . . got this heroin, and that was it.
Brian	That was it, that was't start.
Question	Did you smoke it then, or . . .
Brian	No I injected it.
Question	Straight away?
Brian	Straight away, cos I were injecting speed like first.
Question	Oh right.
Brian	But like er . . .'
Linda	But that were't because o't house weren't it?'
Brian	Yeh, you see like, all't problems through house like. It were a shit tip weren't it?
Linda	Yeh. It were terrible.
Brian	Couldn't use upstairs cos all't rooves had fell in. And t'babby, me and our Linda used to sleep . . .

Linda   We slept on . . . on a scatter cushion . . .

Brian   We slept on one o' them, us, on't floor. That were for 12 month that. And t'babby slept on't settee, didn't she?

Linda   So that's what kept us into heroin that.

Brian   Yeh.

Linda   Because . . . it puts you, like, in Ethiopia at first . . .

Brian   Yeh, it's like . . .

Linda   Ethiopia! . . . [laughs] . . . Utopia . . . Utopia!

Brian   It's just like, you can't get . . . you're just not bothered about nowt then. It's . . . great.

(Linda and Brian, mid-20s, South Yorkshire)

Quite apart from Linda's delicious confusion as to whether heroin had transported her into Utopia or Ethiopia – and maybe at a time when the Ethiopian famine was so much in the news her slip of the tongue betrayed its own set of meanings about a drug that could transform the nightmare of poverty (Ethiopia) into the land of milk and honey (Utopia) – a number of aspects of this brief exchange deserve mention.

First, it seems rather obvious to say that this couple felt some kind of close connection between their poverty and their heroin use. Nevertheless, it would be equally and obviously wrong to say that their wretched housing conditions had 'caused' their heroin use. What stands out most clearly is that their entry into heroin use had an almost accidental character. Heroin would not have been offered to them if they had not already engaged in occasional weekend use of amphetamine sulphate, which meant that they already moved in circles where heroin was just starting to become available in cheap and plentiful supply in the early 1980s. So that one day when 'speed' was not available, they were offered the alternative of 'henry'.

Then, the fact that Brian immediately began to inject heroin – rather than first going through a phase of smoking the drug – appears to be a common pattern where there is already an established practice of injecting amphetamines, either in the individual's own repertoire of drug misuse or in the drug culture of the immediate locality.

But if their heroin use could not be said to have been 'caused' in any meaningful way by their wretched housing difficulties, it immediately offered some kind of 'solution' to their problem. It took away the worries of their appalling situation. 'You weren't bothered about what your house looked like', said Linda, 'You know, it had really been getting me down before . . . I were getting right worked up about it.' And it might also have been experienced as an enormous relief to encounter a drug with the soothing powers of heroin, after being accustomed to the agitated properties of speed – which is not an uncommon experience for someone who moves from 'whizz' to 'smack'.

At first Linda and Brian used heroin weekly, in the same way that they had taken amphetamine on an occasional basis. But whereas their use of speed had assumed a stable pattern of controlled use, they found that they were soon using heroin with increasing regularity. What it offered to this couple was neither a 'buzz' nor a 'hit', but an escape from their housing problems. And as they understood it, it was this which made the continuation of their heroin use more likely once they had been offered it and tried it for the first time. Linda's use of words was very careful: 'That's what *kept us into* heroin', she said, not 'that's what caused it'. And she was quite right. At this second, vital transition point – as someone moves from experimentation to a pattern of regular use – what 'keeps' people into heroin is what matters, because they are not yet addicted. For some it is the pleasure – the 'buzz', the sense of power, the 'wrecked' feeling of being 'gouched out'. For others, it is the ability of heroin to 'solve' their problems, and to cushion them from the world or from themselves.

The Grey Area:
Slippery Slopes and Dabblers

Addiction does not follow on immediately from experimentation and the initial, occasional use of heroin. The rate at which someone does come to depend on heroin probably varies between individuals – at first perhaps taking the form of a 'psychological' dependence, later developing as a physical need if withdrawal sickness is to be avoided; but even so, it will have been necessary to use the drug for some time on a daily basis before the actual onset of a 'habit'. It is common to hear it said, in fact, that you have to work quite hard in order to develop a heroin habit.

Nevertheless, anyone who has begun to experiment with heroin – maybe at first only dabbling with it on an occasional basis – risks the possibility that a pattern of compulsive use will evolve over time, and with it a physical dependence. Sometimes in the recollections of heroin users this experience is passed over in almost no more than a sentence. One young man says:

> 'I just got into it with my mates, and then buying a bag every day . . . and before I knew it, like, I was dependent on it . . . I needed it.' (Malcolm, 23 years, Manchester)

Another remembered how at first he didn't know how to smoke the drug properly, so his first encounters with heroin were not always successful. Even so, this was only a temporary delay in his initiation:

'It took me a while to get hooked really, you know, cos I was sort of . . . I mean I used to sort of blather it. And then that was it – I really got hooked on it. And there was nothing I could do about it.' (Jim, 23 years, Merseyside)

There is a dull monotony in recollections such as these, as if the person concerned had been not only unaware of what was happening, but also somehow uninvolved. Occasionally, however, there is a glimmer of recognition that the person not only was involved, but was also exercising choices on some kind of basis:

'You just don't realise do you? Like you know it's a bad drug when you start with it, like, but you just don't expect to get hooked . . .'
'So you couldn't say that you didn't know what it was?'
'Oh you know what you're doing when you're getting into it, you know what I mean, there's no doubt about it.'
'So why did you carry on?'
'I don't know why . . . You just keep buying it, and buying it . . .' (Billy, 22 years, Manchester)

Wendy from South Yorkshire said something similar:

'You know it's wrong to take . . . but . . . you know, you keep trying again.' (Wendy, 21 years, South Yorkshire)

Abbreviated recollections such as these, although they are quite common, are not terribly helpful if one is trying to reconstruct the early pattern of transitional heroin use, except perhaps as a warning of how rapidly and imperceptibly heroin addiction can sometimes be established. In all probability, however, such accounts gloss over a range of choices and decisions that were made over time.

How to unearth what these choices might have been is not an easy task. The transition by which a person moves from non-addicted occasional or experimental heroin use towards a pattern of habitual use is obviously a crucial milestone in the career of a heroin user, but it will often be characterized by an imperceptible drift. I will call this area of drift the 'grey area', where a person's growing involvement with heroin is unclear and open to widespread misinterpretation – both by themselves and others. For example, as we have already seen, people can become 'hooked' or dependent on heroin without either realizing that this was what was happening or intending that it should happen. But equally, in the early stages of transitional heroin use it is possible for users to believe mistakenly that they are already addicted when in fact they are not. Under these circumstances, they might then identify themselves with the addict lifestyle and pursue the drug as if they were addicted – believing that otherwise they will suffer withdrawal symptoms – with the eventual outcome that they actually do become addicted. What we need to ask in a preliminary way is how people come to assume such mistaken identities, and whether the process is inevitable. Is it possible, in fact, for people to sustain an occasional pattern of heroin use on a recreational basis without becoming addicted?

Early warning: 'It gets your head first'

One of the most powerful, but nevertheless mistaken, aspects of heroin's formidable mythology is that it is instantly addictive. It is certainly true that some people will say that they found heroin to be such a wonderful drug that they 'fell in love' with it immediately. But even so, this is not the same as an instant physical compulsion. Nevertheless, part of heroin's notoriety is its power to enslave and compel, and these beliefs are just as active among heroin users as anywhere else. There is often a contradiction in the views of heroin users towards the drug: on the one hand, it is seen as an enslavement; but on the other, particularly in the early stages of use, people will take the view that they can 'handle it' without succumbing to addiction. It is part of the same ambivalence that we have already noted.

As novice heroin users begin to experiment with the drug, they also begin to learn the 'folklore' of heroin addiction from other, more experienced users. A significant part of this folklore is the experiences of 'turkeying', which will often loom large in the conversational orbit of heroin users, in much the

same way that alcoholics share with each other their experiences of hang-overs. As we shall see later, the experience of
'coming off' heroin is often not nearly as bad as is sometimes
implied by those highly dramatized accounts of the horrors of
'cold turkey' withdrawal in which some ex-addicts trade.
Nevertheless, for novice users who have never experienced
withdrawal, for the simple reason that they are not yet
addicted, what little they will know about 'turkeying' will come
from those tall tales which abound in heroin circles. These
stories revolve a number of typical incidents. So-and-so who
took twenty 'dikeys' at a single sitting and really 'gouched out',
for example, or someone else who was seen 'legging it' from
the law the other day, with half a gram in their pocket, as they
escaped from the clutches of the drug squad who had
suddenly appeared around the corner. And, as a vital centre-
piece to these conversational gambits, recollections of when
there was a 'drought' in the local heroin supply network:
everybody mooching around all day trying to score a 'bag'
when there was none to be found anywhere, and 'turkeying
real bad'.

In these ways the novice user will learn among other things
the necessity of avoiding withdrawal sickness, although this
learning might be quite inappropriate to his or her actual level
of drug involvement if someone has not yet developed a
'habit'. One ex-user in Liverpool described from his own
experience, and from that of other novice users whom he had
known, how an inappropriate belief that one needed to take
heroin in order to avoid withdrawal sickness could become a
self-fulfilling prophecy which would lead to eventual addiction:

'I think people get the wrong ideas, y'know, people who've
just started on it . . . And they've smoked it for a month or
two months, or what have you, and then they haven't got it
one day. Well, alright, you know, they might feel a bit
rough. But they start, y'know . . . they've got it in their
heads that they're going through withdrawal symptoms. So
they're out to get more to make them feel that bit better
because they were feeling rough . . . and before you know
it, they *are* hooked on it.' (Paul, 24 years, Merseyside)

A young woman from another part of Merseyside put it this way:

> 'You get some of them, what haven't been into it that long . . . but they're hanging round with a crowd who are really into it, like. And they want to be part of it, you know part of the smack-head scene . . . they don't really know what's going on, but they're trying to get accepted like. And, er, they're going, "Oh I'm turkeying real bad" and all that, "Oh you should've seen me this morning" . . . But they're not. They don't know what a turkey is . . . it's like play-acting. You know what I mean? Well, I think it is anyway.' (Gail, 20 years, Merseyside)

It may seem strange to an outsider that someone would wish to be accepted with a circle of heroin users in this way. But when the drug has started to become a central focus of a neighbourhood's youth culture, as it can do, then being a 'smack-head' can even assume something of a heroic status. Even the notoriety that attaches to heroin can then be enjoyed:

> 'People had to take notice of me, like. Suddenly I was someone round here . . . Jack the Lad . . . before that I'd been a nobody.' (Alan, 21 years, Lancashire)

And for the novice user there can be other reasons for wishing to be identified with, and accepted by, the local heroin network:

> 'You do get these who've hardly got into it, but they start coming on big . . . like real addicts, you know. And they're not even baby addicts, you know what I mean? They know nothing . . . what the crack is like. They're pathetic . . . But I remember, when we were just getting into it, just buying a £5 wrap now and again, sometimes you'd try and buy some . . . and if there wasn't a lot around, say, you'd be trying to buy some and you'd get told to fuck off. You know, "Fuck off you, you don't really need it" kind of thing. And so, you start acting up like you're really into it, when you weren't . . . you were just dabbling in it. And then, after a time, you start to believe it yourself. Honest to God, it's weird.' (Colin, 23 years, Manchester)

Another way in which these early identifications with the heroin scene are sometimes remembered, prior to the actual onset of a physical dependence, is to say that heroin became a 'psychological' need. Linda and Brian from South Yorkshire, who first started using heroin only on a weekly basis, had this to say about their earliest experiences:

Linda   But like, even that gets to be an habit . . . having it every week.

Brian   You don't realise it, but it does.

Linda   And then it just . . . became more and more, then . . .

Brian   Yeh. Twice a week, three times a week, then it got to every day like. And then . . .

Linda   It gets to your head first, psychologically, it gets your head first before it's physical.

Brian   You're not addicted to it physically . . . you need it, like, but it's in your head . . .

(Linda and Brian, mid-20s, South Yorkshire)

Some people would say, no doubt, that Linda and Brian were mistaken and that they had become physically dependent on heroin without realizing it. But they were quite sure on the basis of their experience that the physical withdrawal symptoms, which they did subsequently come to suffer after about six months of continuous use, were completely different from these earlier feelings of 'psychological' dependence. Eddie from Merseyside would agree:

'When you get hooked on it you get, sort of, psychologically hooked at first. Do you know what I mean? You're saying, "I *need* this . . . I need it", like . . . and you don't. But you buy it again, and then one day you just wake up and you're fucked. Pains all over like, and you go, "I've got a . . . head", like that you know. "Where am I going to get my money from now?" Mooching about, buying it, and you just get worse and worse . . .' (Eddie, 21 years, Merseyside)

The question of occasional use: 'Oh I can handle it'

What does all this add up to? Does it mean that, by one route or another, someone who dabbles in heroin will inevitably become addicted eventually? Or is it that these particular people suffered from a 'weakness' of will-power? Extensive research in North America suggests that patterns of controlled opiate use on an occasional recreational basis, known in the USA as 'chipping', are in fact much more common than compulsive, addicted use (cf. Zinberg, 1984). The difference between controlled opiate users and compulsive users, as described by Zinberg and his colleagues, is that the controlled users adhere to strict rules on the frequency of use – using heroin only on a very occasional basis, or on special occasions, and never on consecutive days. Non-compulsive users are also more likely to have a variety of other valued commitments in their lives, such as family and work responsibilities, as well as recreational pursuits which conflict with regular opiate use. They will also tend to have access to a knowledgeable network of controlled users who can offer advice and support to the novice on such such matters as the frequency of use that is deemed safe, or when the beginning user's pattern of drug use might look as if it threatens to get out of control.

Other research in North America, by Stanton Peele (1985), confirms this general impression while at the same time stressing the social-psychological basis of addictive experiences which he considers to be more important than their physical basis. Peele's view is that people become addicted to *activities* rather than to *substances*, pointing to the compulsive behaviour which is sometimes associated with practices such as gambling, food intake or even the pursuit of physical fitness. The work of Zinberg and Peele differ in certain respects, although they also point in a common direction. What distinguishes non-compulsive drug users is that they:

'subordinate their desire for the drug to other values, activities and personal relationships, so that the narcotic or other drug does not dominate their lives. When engaged in other pursuits that they value, these users do not crave the drug or manifest withdrawal on discontinuing their drug use.' (Peele, 1985, p. 8)

Small-scale research in Britain has identified similar features within the lifestyles of controlled opiate users (cf. Blackwell, 1983). It also showed how people who had used heroin on a recreational basis over a period of time would sometimes take action to discontinue or regulate their drug use if they felt that it was drifting out of control towards dependence. The problems which motivated people to take such action included the following:

> 'Loss of appetite, irregular sleep patterns, needle marks and spotty complexions . . . Two respondents said that they stopped using in order to get into shape for the football season.' (Blackwell, 1983, p. 228)

What seems remarkable is that, given the common view of heroin as a totally enslaving preoccupation, such a humdrum reason as 'getting into shape for the football season' could motivate someone to stop using the drug. Generally speaking, however, this British research tends to confirm the view of Zinberg and Peele from North America that for the controlled use of opiates to be sustained over any length of time there must be other commitments in a person's life which compete with the claims of heroin.

Now, to return to the heroin users and ex-users whom we have been listening to, what would they say to such a proposition? When asked whether they knew of any people who were able to control heroin use on a recreational or weekend basis, the answer was invariably 'No'. For example:

> 'No. I've never met anybody, unless they're first getting into it. Then you can take it and leave it. You get these ones, like, who say, "Oh I can handle it". You know. But they can't. They're just like everyone else, aren't they?' (Gail, 20 years, Merseyside)

> 'I've seen loads of people do it like that, but as I say, three months later . . . not for a long period . . . I've seen people do it for two or three months, take it here and there, but I've seen the same people three months later and they're just wrecked on it. And before they know it . . . because it just comes up on you, and before you know it, you're on it. Really on it.' (Ronnie, 21 years, Manchester)

The question could even be the occasion for a grim kind of mirth:

'Do you know anybody who uses it occasionally, who can just use it at weekends, that kind of thing?'

'[Laughs] . . . You just smoke it every time you get yer hands on it, you just smoke it . . . know what I mean, if you're into it . . . You must be joking! It gets in your blood . . . it gets in your hair, your hair's all greasy . . . it gets in your brain and in your sweat . . . Did you know some people say that you can tell a smackhead by the way they smell? Did you know that?' (Gavin, 22 years, Merseyside)

'What? Take it and leave it? . . . [laughs] . . . Where've *you* been? Honest to God, you come up with some barmy bloody questions, you do!' (Colin, 23 years, Manchester)

These dismissive answers seem emphatic enough. But behind the unqualified denial, it would sometimes appear that perhaps the question had not been properly understood. It was immediately assumed, in fact, that what was being asked was whether someone could use heroin regularly on a daily basis and still keep it under control – which is not the point at issue, because daily heroin use will inevitably lead to addiction. What, then, do these answers actually mean?

Sometimes the form that someone's answer took was that it would quickly shift from a general consideration of the possibility of occasional heroin use, to that of the user's own experience of decline:

'Do you know any people who just use it now and then?'

'Yeh, there is too. Some people are like that . . . well at first they are.'

'How many people have you known like that?'

'I've known a few in the past like, that just used to take it and leave it . . . I was sort of like that when I first got into it, I could take it and leave it, but eventually it fucking gets hold of you and that's it . . . "I'm never gonna be hooked" and that, like . . . Well, I fucking was good on . . . in no time.' (Eddie, 21 years, Merseyside)

There might even sometimes be a fleeting acknowledgement
that heroin need not be addictive if it was only used seldomly,
but this was not given any prominence in a person's answer,
which would quickly give way to a description of the hazards
of daily use:

'You can take it every week cos it's not addictive then, like,
is it? But if you take it every day, no, you haven't got it
under control. Take it every day like for three weeks . . . you
need it, that's it then. I'd say . . . three weeks, if you get
wrecked every night for three weeks I'd say you're addicted.
It's so easy, really it is. No I don't know anyone that can
control it.' (John, 19 years, Merseyside)

'People kid themselves, you kid yourself like, about not
turkeying and that. But you only leave it a couple of hours.
You go and buy a smoke, straight away like, and never give
yourself a chance to turkey.' (Joey, 20 years, Merseyside)

What these answers seem to indicate is that there is not the
faintest recognition that daily use is not the only option, or
what safeguards might be observed in order to limit one's
involvement with the drug. 'Controlled' heroin use, along the
lines of the North American 'chipping' model, is not what this
new working class heroin culture in Britain is about. The drug
culture into which the novice heroin user moves, then
beginning to learn its ways, is interested only in getting
wrecked every day, day in and day out. So that even when one
ex-user did remember someone whom he knew, who clearly
could sustain a pattern of very occasional heroin use, his
reaction was simply one of puzzlement:

'Do you know anyone who can control it, or just use it at
weekends, or anything like that?

'No . . . [laughs] . . . They try to kid, like, that they've got
it under control. But there's no way you can control it, is
there?

'So there's no-one round here who . . . '

'Oh, I'll tell you. There is one mate, his brother, he used to
have it. And there'd be nights when he'd have loads and
loads, but he could just . . . I don't know what it was. He

must be able to just switch himself off in the day, like, the next day after he'd had a big load . . . just felt alright like. I can't understand it. Like, he never turkeyed or nothing like that. I just couldn't understand it . . . [long pause] . . . Some people must have . . . their bodies must be different or something. The withdrawal must react different to different people like.' (Jack, 22 years, Merseyside)

Jack was quite unable to see that it was the frequency and pattern of this man's heroin use which enabled him to 'take it and leave it'. Instead, he invoked some kind of biological speculation – 'their bodies must be different or something' – in order to account for what he saw. It is possibly true that different people do have different reactions to opiates at a physiological level, but this was not what is being described to us here. Rather, it is a pattern of heroin use on rare occasions, similar to that identified by Norman Zinberg in the North American 'chipping' culture, which can be sustained without leading to compulsive use. Jack's recollection was that this acquaintance used 'loads and loads' during his occasional bouts, although that cannot have been quite true because a 'chipper's' tolerance to heroin would be low. Indeed, a major risk of this kind of single-bout heroin use is the possibility of overdose, because the user has not established a tolerance against a properly estimated purity of the drug. What is more likely is that this mate's brother had 'loads and loads' of money to spend within the local heroin economy, because he was in work among people who were not. And this carries its own risks, as a number of people have found to their cost. Because with money in your pocket, and with so much largesse to spread among a group of heroin-using acquaintances in an impoverished neighbourhood, it is also possible to develop an excessive appetite for the drug, to spend large amounts of money in a short time, run up huge bills, and maybe pick up a heroin habit along the way.

Absent claims: drug cultures and unemployment

Unemployment is undoubtedly one major reason why patterns

of occasional, recreational use have not established themselves within the new heroin culture in working-class neighbour-hoods, and why instead one finds runaway forms of daily use which can quickly assume an epidemic form. This is something which could have been easily predicted from the North American experience of the 1950s and the 1960s, where the most serious problems of heroin misuse tended to gather together in areas of high economic and social deprivation, such as the ghettos of New York, Chicago and elsewhere (cf. Chein et al., 1964; Feldman, 1968; Preble and Casey, 1969; Hughes, 1977; Johnson et al., 1985). It is also something which would follow from the explorations by Zinberg and Peele into 'con-trolled' opiate use, which have identified the vital importance of other valued and sustaining commitments that can compete with the claims of heroin in the lives of non-compulsive users. In areas of high unemployment, one of the most important forms of life commitment – namely, a work identity – is an absent claim.

The experience of the North American ghettos has also shown how within the social void of poverty and unemploy-ment, alternative lifestyles came to be fashioned around heroin which could bring with them social rewards such as self-esteem and status within the local community. The lifestyle of the street addict, as described by such writers as Ed Preble and James Casey from New York, requires a great deal of resourcefulness, energy and sharp wits. It is not in all respects the passive, escapist lifestyle that is so often imagined. The euphoric lethargy that might be occasioned by a heroin 'high' is only a small part of the user's otherwise busy day. The street user is engaged in a constant flurry of activity, knowing who is who on the heroin scene; who is selling the best bag and where to buy it; who to avoid if you don't want to get 'ripped off'; constantly hustling for the money to buy the next bag; and above all, steering clear of the law.

As the novice user first enters the world of heroin, this active addict lifestyle can sometimes prove as attractive and exciting as the effects of the drug itself – offering one further, compelling enticement to deepen one's involvement with the drug culture. And something similar to this pattern described from the North American ghettos may be beginning to emerge in some of the impoverished and embattled communities of unemployed Britain.

Unemployment is not only a financial blight upon people's lives. It also brings with it a variety of effects upon people's lifestyles, their psychology and their self-identity. It is through employment that people gain access to a wider set of social involvements, friendships and activities than would otherwise be the case. Employment status confers major elements of self-esteem in a society such as ours, and it is also the basis of meaningful time-structures which order a person's daily routines. Research conducted both during the Slump of the 1930s and the current economic recession identifies the question of how to cope with the destruction of habitual time-structures and routines as one of the most difficult problems faced by unemployed people (cf. Jahoda, 1972 and 1982). Heroin and its accompanying lifestyle in this context can help people to fill their day and to 'kill' time. And, of course, without the binding obligations of employment routines, there is absolutely no reason why heroin should remain merely an occasional, recreational pursuit.

Wendy	I mean, we've known people round here, haven't we who just dabble in it . . . use it at weekends, that kind of thing.
Cheryl	That's how they usually start off, isn't it, like just having it at weekends.
Question	How is it, then, that some people end up . . .
Cheryl	They just carry on like.
Question	But why?
Mother	I think . . . Don't you think you've got to put it this way. People what are working, if they've got good sense, they've got sommat to look out for. They're not gonna take it, are they, through't week when they're going to work. Where as you get somebody what's in't unemployed, they'll have it at weekend and they'll continue wi' it, cos they've got nowt else to do have they? Because you do get sensible people like that, don't you, if they're working they just . . . they'll not bother

wi' it through't week. Well that's how I see it.
(Cheryl and Wendy, early 20s, South Yorkshire)

As a brisk summary of what is known about the complex psychology of unemployment, Cheryl's mother had hit the nail right on the head. Although the problem also runs deeper than that, because in those areas where unemployment reaches such levels that it becomes the exception rather than the rule to be in work, then even for those who are in work the value attached to employment status can become eroded. Barry, for example, is a young man who lives on a small council estate on the outskirts of Manchester, in a town ravaged by unemployment. In his immediate locality at the time when heroin first started to become available, only a tiny handful of people in his age group were in work. He started using heroin along with a group of friends, and at first he enjoyed a pattern of occasional use on a weekend basis. He did not become addicted: during the week he did not feel any compulsion to the use the drug, although his appetite for heroin grew enormously during his weekend bouts. But eventually, he found to his cost that his pattern of recreational use came to rest uneasily against the lifestyle of his unemployed companions. Before long, he abandoned his commitment to work in favour of the lifestyle of his friends:

'I had this job, a good job, y'know. Bringing in the money, £120 a week, when there weren't that many jobs around . . . well not around here, anyway. I liked to have a few pints with the lads, that kind of thing. A lot of my mates were on the dole, good lads, you know, and we'd see 'em through the week like. Buy 'em a drink now and then, when I could see my way. Then the heroin came round, and some fellas I knew were using it. At first I thought, fuck that, you know; heroin? no way. But they seemed alright on it, and I thought I'd give it a try . . . see what the crack was, you know. And it was okay, I liked it.

'What do you mean?'

It was just . . . whoosh . . . an instant hit, you know, like the best high ever. So, I got into it a bit . . . just at weekends though, cos I had to be up early in the morning for work and that. Anyway, I was having a right good time. Still working, bringing in the money, getting blasted at the weekend. But . . . well, it got that way, I was using that much . . . you know, smoking a hell of a lot at the weekend, that I was broke on Monday morning. Paid on Thursday, broke on Monday like. All through the week, no money . . . I wasn't turkeying or any of that, but I thought "Fuck this for a lark". All the lads I knew were on the dole like . . . I mean nearly everyone round here's on the dole, you know what I mean . . . and they were just running around, just taking smack all week, having a toot here and there like, some of them doing a bit of dealing . . . just one to another, you know, getting by one way and another. And there I was, sweating my guts out at work . . . no fun; no money cos I'd blown it all at the weekend. Well, I went on like for a bit, but I was getting right pissed off. So I just . . . eventually I just jacked the job in, like. Just said, fuck that, you know. Joined in with the rest of the lads, you know, just going for the smack. Taking it every day. I was soon knackered like the rest of 'em . . . but there you go.' (Barry, 22 years, Manchester)

Friendship Falls Apart

In the 'grey area' of transitional heroin use, the extent to which someone is becoming more deeply involved with the drug is open to a variety of forms of misinterpretation. Indeed, it is not always possible to disentangle the different strands of a person's involvement. For some, the novelty and excitement of the heroin user's lifestyle can at first seem the main attraction. For others, where heroin is beginning to be used widely among their friends, it is friendship which draws them closer towards a potentially dangerous level of involvement. Others describe a 'psychological' entanglement with heroin, which probably includes these attractions of lifestyle and friendship. As they pass through the 'grey area', people will also sometimes believe mistakenly that they have already become addicted and continue to use the drug for fear of withdrawal symptoms, with the eventual outcome of course that they do become addicted. But an equally dangerous kind of 'mistaken identity' is when addiction follows on so swiftly and imperceptibly that someone does not believe that they are addicted, when in fact they are.

The slide into habitual use: 'I'd better be careful with this'

'It was weird. I always said, everyone says like, I won't get hooked on it, and you never think you will . . . you never think it will happen to you. I was having it every day, and I was thinking to myself, "Oh, I'll have to be careful with this". Cos when I first started having it most of my mates were addicts then, like, so I knew what it could do to people. I thought, "I'd better be careful with this" . . . So I'd had it every day, a bit every day . . . this was just a bag with two mates, and I'd say to myself, "I'd better just not have none and see what happens", to see if I'd start turkeying. And I'd leave it for a full day, and I'd feel OK and I'd think, "Oh I must be alright then, I'm not turkeying". So I'd go and have it the next day. And it'd go on like that for weeks. Until, finally, I left it for two days and on the second day I just started, really bad, turkeying like . . . All I can say is it must have taken a whole 24 hours to get out of my system before I started turkeying, because on the second, I was really bad, like, I can't understand it . . . I thought, "Shit".' (Jack, 22 years, Merseyside)

Jack's story is not only typical of a common pattern of the transition into habitual use, where heroin users initially deny that they will become addicted and are then overtaken by events, his experience is also instructive in a number of other ways. He was not ignorant of what the drug could do to people, because he had the example of his friends before him who had become addicted earlier. Indeed, he had been offered heroin on a number of occasions by friends over a two year period before he eventually tried it, and had always refused the offer.

'But it had been there for years before I tried it. I remember two years before I ever got into it, a mate of mine was having it, and he'd offer it to me than. I was scared like, "No way, I'm not touching that", like. But two years later that's when I started, gradually sort of come round . . . and the next minute it was everywhere, like. It just sort of took Liverpool by storm.'

A great deal of play has been made with the slogan, 'Just Say No' in recent months and years. But the fact that someone initially refuses an offer of heroin from friends does not in any way guarantee that they will go on refusing in the future. Wendy from South Yorkshire had a similar experience:

> ' . . . I always used to refuse it, and then once I said yeh.' (Wendy, 21 years, South Yorkshire)

And so did Josephine:

> 'My boyfriend's friends were all using it and that, and giving it to me . . . They were always offering me chases, and I was refusing it, but then I gradually slipped into it.' (Josephine, 28 years, Humberside)

Indeed, for one young man, heroin had at first been such a totally alien phenomenon that he could not identify with it at all, except through the imagery of American gangster movies:

> 'I'd never dream of me taking heroin. Like, heroin was . . . to me before I was on it, it was . . . just a *word*, you know, that I used to see on films and that. You know, you used to see these yankees in the street, the junkies buying their gear, needles hanging out of their arms . . . that was what heroin was to me. Do you know what I mean? I'd have never even *dreamed* I'd have ever took it or been on it . . . The first few times I seen my mates doing it, having a toot whatever, I was amazed. Like, "What the fuck are you doing?" I imagined they'd be . . . oh I don't know . . . running around with bloody great guns or something next, you know blasting each other's heads away . . . like in the films, you know? You didn't really expect to see that kind of thing around our area. It was all beer and darts, and a bit of draw and that was the limit. I said, "No way" . . .' (Arthur, 24 years, Manchester)

So, Jack's initial reluctance to try heroin was by no means exceptional. What, then, of the elementary precautions which he had tried to take against the possibility of becoming addicted when he did eventually start to use heroin, by occasionally abstaining from use? These, of course, were deeply flawed. What Jack clearly did not know is that where patterns of stable, non-addicted opiate use on a recreational basis have been identified (as in the North American 'chipping' culture which I discussed briefly in the last chapter), these are only sustained if people adhere to strict rules about the frequency of use. And one of these rules, invariably, is that the drug is only taken very occasionally, and *never* on consecutive days. If heroin is used on a daily basis over a period of weeks, as Jack used it, then an addiction will follow as surely as night follows day.

It is of course impossible to know whether Jack would have been able to sustain a pattern of occasional use, even if he had been supplied with effective advice of this kind. But without it, he stood no chance whatsoever. What is more certain is that street-hoardings and television videos telling him that 'Heroin Screws You Up' would have made little difference to his drug choices. He had watched from close quarters while it screwed up his friends, and yet he had still eventually decided to try heroin, whereupon the process which he had observed in his friends' lives would be repeated in his own subsequent experiences with the drug:

'I got sick of the smack as well, but what's the worst part of it . . . you grow up with your mates, you know through school and all that, and then you see them change with the smack. They're all trying to . . . just trying to con you all the time. And you think, "Fucking hell, this is weird", y'know your mates trying to con you . . . So I got sick of that. I just stayed in. I must have stayed in for about six months . . . only time I went out was when I went out to score for some gear . . .'

This, moreover, stood in sharp contrast to Jack's former lifestyle and recreational pursuits:

'Like, I used to be the one, though, for y'know . . . I used to go out every Wednesday, Thursday, Friday, Saturday and Sunday like, to a club. All the time, copping off with loads of girls all the time, one of those guys who loves going out and all that . . . And I just stopped going out completely. For the past two years I didn't go to a pub at all like. Not once. I just changed completely, I just didn't go out. Just sat in, just stayed in the house all the time. Never bothered to go out and have one drink. Even now I can't drink ale.'

This appears to be once more a typical way in which heroin
users recollect both their growing involvement with the drug
and the damage which was brought with it into their lives – as
something which was most significantly measured by the way
in which their friendships began to fall apart. Sometimes, of
course, the break up of friendships would be part of an active
disengagement from one's former life and a repudiation of its
values:

> 'My school mates, if I seen 'em I didn't want to know
> 'em . . . they were plastics cos they didn't take smack.'
> (Cheryl, 20 years, South Yorkshire)

Even so, as people recollected their experiences with heroin,
the drift into habitual use was often measured against the
deterioration of their previously established friendships and
recreational patterns. And this might have been especially so
for young men:

> 'I've known really good lads who I've known for years, grew
> up with, and I've known 'em to be really good lads, who'd
> give you their last sort of thing, help yer out. And I've just
> seen 'em change completely. I mean in this heroin game
> there's a lot of back-stabbers. You can't trust no-one. Cos
> everyone'll pull a stroke if it means getting gear and all.
> There's no such thing as friendship.' (Ronnie, 21 years,
> Manchester)

This kind experience was described in different ways, time and
time again:

> 'There was a few of us, and we were all good mates and that
> like, and we all tried it . . . and then eventually everyone
> was just, got hooked on it. So like, we were all just . . . like
> we all just went dead weird to one another . . . Fuck you,
> like . . . We weren't interested. I lost interest in my family,
> my girl and everything like . . . my ma and dad have split
> up . . . and I've even got fines now to pay . . .'
> 'How quickly did all that happen?'
> 'It just crept up on me . . . it catches up with you like . . .
> I *really* went down . . . right down . . . I was near enough in
> the grids, y'know, I was that down . . . you lose weight and

everything like that, I'm just sort of getting my features back again. I even got into my kid sister's jeans, 28 waist, 27 waist . . . eats your muscles away and everything, batters your brain . . . there's a lot of things to do with it.' (Eddie, 21 years, Merseyside)

'I haven't been out for a pint since . . . oh I don't know when. I've never known a smackhead go to pubs, never. It was . . . if you've got £15 to go out for the night, you're not going to spend it on ale. If someone says, "Here y'are, are you coming out?" and you've got £15 you'd say "No", go and buy three bags. I don't know anyone that'd rather go out than take it.' (Kevin, 21 years, Merseyside)

'I stopped going to football . . . and I used to love football, you know, the match. I stopped going to concerts, going out like. That was it . . .' (Billy, 22 years, Manchester)

'Before the smack came round, what I really liked was going to concerts and what have you . . . It's good that, if you get a draw and that, and go down and get into it, have a good night out . . . yeh, a good night out . . . I could do with one o' them now, like. It's nice to be, know what I mean, at the Empire when there's a good band or something, you can really get into it . . . But, argh, like the smackheads . . . "Argh, fuck this" or something, "I'm not buying that ticket" like, "I can get a bag" . . .' (Gavin, 22 years, Merseyside)

Families and values:
'It affects people who don't even take it'

Often, as in these recollections, the heroin user's drift through the 'grey area' into habitual use was remembered simply as a movement away from former friends and recreations, and would be described as a total condemnation of the heroin user's lifestyle. But at other times it was not only what was identified as a withdrawal from an active engagement with the world that was regretted, but also the effect of one's behaviour on one's immediate family:

'Before I was on it, I used to love going for a bevvy and

going to clubs and what have you. But when you get on that, you just don't socialize at all. You just sort of hibernate . . . You get yer gear, you'll either go home or go to someone's house or whatever, just smoke yer gear and stay in . . . just don't bother. I mean there's a lot of things that you just stop doing. You just lose interest in everything. You don't care about nothing or nobody. And it's not just like you, the user, it affects. It affects yer family, y'know what I mean . . . It affects people who don't even take it.' (Paul, 24 years, Merseyside)

Given the typical image of a heroin addict as someone utterly divorced from conventional standards and values, it is important to recognize that people not uncommonly expressed a deep attachment to their families, and particularly as far as young men were concerned to their mothers. Indeed, this registers one of the most significant differences between the new heroin users and the former generation. For whereas heroin use from the late 1960s and through the 1970s was largely confined to London's 'West End' Piccadilly scene and the vaguely bohemian culture of bed-sit communities such as Notting Hill, the new heroin users are much more likely to come from intact families with whom they have retained close links, even if these often become strained:

'Oh, my mam . . . she was shattered like and everything when she found out. She was really deep . . . you know, she was down for days and that like, and I just tried to tell her, like, that I was getting off it . . . Like, so she thinks I have been off it now for a good few months, you know since that day when I went to the hospital . . . since just after that she thinks I've been off it. But it's only been four weeks now, you know . . . I was, sort, trying to protect her like.'

'Did she ever go to a parents' groups or anything like that?'

'No, I don't think there's any of them parents' groups around here, like . . . It'd be interesting to, like, listen to them, you know, to see what they think . . . I really feel bad about my mam.' (Jack, 22 years, Merseyside)

And again:

'I've done some horrible things . . . really, I have. Robbed
from my mam and things like that. And when I moved back
to our house, you know my ma she's great and everything,
but . . . I'd just say I'm going upstairs and put the record on,
and she'd know I was taking it, you know the smack. But
she was . . . trying to convince herself I wasn't, you know
what I mean, she wouldn't come up and catch me. She
could've sneaked up and caught me, cos I got caught by my
brothers and that . . . but my ma always made a noise
coming up. Shouted, "Jimmy, what you're doing?" to me,
you know, before she walked in . . . And I'd just turn round
and say "Nothing" like . . . She could've just pulled back the
quilt and seen it all. But she didn't want to. She told me,
she'd never like . . . she knows I take it, and how I take it
like, but she never . . . she said, if she ever seed me now
with a tube in my mouth . . . degrading she thinks it is. She
reckons it'd kill her. Cos she's . . . since I've gone on it,
she's nearly . . . near to a nervous breakdown and everything. I wanted to stop it, but there was nothing I could do
about it . . . It's horrible . . . horrible it was.' (Jim, 23 years,
Merseyside)

' . . . the way I treated my mam, like, I mean that's as low as
you can get. I just didn't care. You just don't know what
you're doing like . . . And when I got stuck away, you read
some o' the letters and all that what she wrote . . . brilliant.
You sit there in jail, thinking . . . you know what I mean,
"How come she's writing letters like this?" when I've done
all that I have. Oh it's brilliant.' (John, 19 years, Merseyside)

If it was not uncommon for heroin users and ex-users to
lament the effect which their drug use had had on their
families, they would also express other forms of conventional
values such as a feeling that it was wrong for young women to
use heroin:

'You know, it just doesn't seem right somehow. I don't like
to see girls getting involved . . . I don't like to see a girl

using smack. They do, though.' (Colin, 23 years, Manchester)

One young woman who did use heroin described how this had resulted in a breakup with her boyfriend as a result of her sense of shame, mingled with a feeling that she must try to protect him:

> 'Like I said, he'd been working away and wrote to say he'd be coming home. And, you know, I tried to get off it, but it didn't work . . . Well, then when he did come home I just avoided him. I mean, I was really keen on him. But . . . well, I felt so ashamed, you know? I didn't want him to see me like that. And, I don't know, I didn't want to see him getting involved in heroin, so . . . I don't think he would have got involved, but then again you can't say . . . So that was it.' (June, 22 years, Manchester)

June lost a boyfriend as a result of heroin. For Linda and Brian, on the other hand, it was the loss of what they described as their spiritual life which they most regretted:

> Linda We were spiritual, like, reet spiritual before heroin came along. You know what I mean?
> Brian Aye, long before . . .
> Linda But when that come along, it takes . . . it cuts your emotions down.
> Brian Yeh, it just stops you feeling.
> Linda You know, it just changes *you* as a person completely, to somebody else . . . You know, there's somebody else in your body. It's not you at all . . .
> (Linda and Brian, mid-20s, South Yorkshire)

If there is again a somewhat dull uniformity in so many of the things which these people seem to be saying about their involvement with heroin – the loss of emotion, the dislocation of friendship, the effect on their families, the disruption of their previous recreational pursuits – it is nevertheless important to recognize that these same things were being said by otherwise quite different kinds of people. So that whereas for Linda and Brian it was the effect on their spiritual beliefs which they came to regret, for another young man his growing

involvement with heroin was measured against the loss of a
far-from-spiritual lifestyle:

> 'I used to have a pot and all that. I *do* like that, good to relax
> on. It's not addictive and that like, you can take it and leave
> it . . . And I used to love the speed, then, and we used to
> buy it like I bought smack at first . . . I'd buy it off a
> weekend if I was going out to town, just to perk me up and
> keep me going, sort of before you can get pissed and that,
> and have a draw with it and that . . . and that was a good
> night out like . . . chasin' women all over town . . . You just
> forget all of that, like, it just does you right in. Just stay in
> and all of that, you know totally wiped in . . .'
> 'You mean before you took heroin, although you were
> using other drugs, you could control that . . . just at
> weekends, and that was fun?'
> 'It is. That's good, like if you've got your mates and all
> that . . . And I can remember, when we used to go to town
> and that, and like it's just different now . . . [very bitterly]
> . . . it just died . . .'
> 'There was no place for that and heroin?'
> 'That's it man.' (Gavin, 22 years, Merseyside)

Gavin was clearly no angel before he got into heroin, but
again it was a form of established friendship which he
experienced as the greatest cost of his involvement with the
drug, and this was a uniform pattern in so many of these
accounts of the slippery slope movement through the 'grey
area' of transitional use. This change of lifestyle might have
been originally experienced as both new and exciting, although
this was almost always remembered as something which
eventually gave way to a dull compulsion:

> 'When the heroin first came round, there was a few into
> it . . . just a few . . . and they were, you know, the elite.
> And I just wanted to get into that, like. It was, I don't know,
> Jack the Lad . . . do you know what I mean? And then,
> well . . . you just got into chasing a bag here and there,
> always chasing a bag . . .'
> 'What, that was a bit of a bore?'

'Oh no. At first, it was . . . like I said, the best thing ever. Deffo. I mean the smack was good stuff then as well, really good stuff. Now it's *last* . . . you know what I mean, brick-dust and all that kind of shit in it . . . Anyway there was me and this lad, like, and we were really getting into it, when everyone else was just . . . left behind, y'know. And, er, we were like the elite, the cream . . . Everyone used to look up to us, as the one's who could really handle it . . . Running here and there, getting a bag. But then it just . . . got to you, like. It just wasn't fun anymore. Like, one minute we were the elite, the next minute we were just like any other scraggy arsed smackhead . . . [laughs] . . . y'know what I mean?'

'How long was that?'

'Oh, I don't know, I really couldn't tell you to be honest. Now . . . well, it seems like no time at all. Then, it seemed like ages. I don't know . . . three months?' (Michael, 21 years, Merseyside)

Indeed, whichever way it was phrased, the process was invariably remembered as something which slipped by imperceptibly:

'I had a job and everything, and I had a lot of money . . . just you know, like I had plenty o' money and all that so I just tried it. And then, just carried on taking it for about three months. And then I was addicted before I knew it . . . I was using so much, I didn't have a chance to turkey or nothing like that. If I had've turkeyed, I would've stopped . . .'

'Was that with friends?'

'Yeh. All my mates. At first we'd go down to an away match, like down against Aston Villa. And then we just had a go that night. And then we just started getting it . . . But I started off too strong. Most of 'em started off with £5 worth a day. I started on a quarter of a gram a day. That was the second time I took it. And the third time I took it, I took £50 a day, one day . . . Oh, I did, I collapsed. Just woke up, and didn't know what I was doing'

'Did you carry on with the football?'

'No.'

'What, did it drop off straight away?'

'Yeh, just packed in going to the match. As soon as I started, you know I packed it in. Yeh . . . it just took over . . . everything.'

'How long was it before you knew you had a problem?'

'Only three months . . . at the most. Y'see, I just took it every night. I used to take at least half a gram a night, you know £35. And then I just said one night, I'll leave it cos I had something else to do. I was going to see somebody that's the girlfriend's cousin, and I didn't want to make a show of her or nothin' . . . So, I got home from work at five, you know after like, I hadn't been turkeying all day or nothin'. And it was just that . . . when I got home from work . . . "Here y'are I'll go and get some now before I go to this" . . . Y'know I couldn't . . . like, I felt as if I was tripping. Everything was blurry, like. I don't know . . . just felt dead weird and everything until I took some again. So . . . then, I had to take it every night until I got registered.' (John, 19 years, Merseyside)

Grim and relentless: 'Like a black cloud'

There is sometimes a frightening rapidity in the ease with which, as people recollect events, they had developed a heroin habit. And yet this is not the same as saying that heroin is an 'instant fix' which exerts an immediate pharmacological enslavement over people. On the contrary, what these voices from the street seem to be saying to us is that the heroin experience is more insidious than that, edging itself into their lives by imperceptible degrees. Heroin's advance is not like some sudden cavalry charge; more like the slow trudge of a foot army. 'Junk wins by default' is how William Burroughs (1977, p. xv) described it thirty years ago.

There are, as we have seen, sometimes sharp inconsistencies in the accounts which people give of their involvement with heroin. It is something which can come to be understood as a swift current in their lives. Although this recollection of events was often betrayed by the slow, movement as the events themselves had unfolded. Linda and Brian's experiences exemplify this sometimes muddled timescale particularly well – in that theirs was a relentless, creeping involvement with heroin which was nevertheless sometimes remembered as a sudden lurch. Their initial experience with the drug was in some ways different to that of many others of the new users whom we have enountered. They first injected heroin, for example, rather than smoking it. Their pattern of consumption was also modest in comparison with those who might smoke as much half a gram or a whole gram per day. But in other respects, their experiences were the same: what had started out as a pleasurable experimentation ended as a painful episode in their lives.

Married, now in their mid-twenties with a child, we last met Linda and Brian in their grim house, which was falling down about their ears, where they had first encountered heroin (or 'henry' as Brian called it) almost accidentally. Heroin, it will be remembered, at first appeared to offer them some kind of 'solution' to their housing problem, transporting Linda into 'Utopia' – or was it 'Ethiopia'? Now, three years after their creeping involvement with heroin began, they are engaged in another kind of trudging infantry movement, slowly trying to reduce their intake of methadone which is prescribed for them by their local psychiatric clinic.

Before Linda and Brian first encountered heroin, as we have seen, they had experimented with amphetamine sulphate and also smoked cannabis.

Linda	Just blow we'd had before, hadn't we, and then just a bit of sulph weren't it?
Brian	Yeh, just the odd line now and again, you know.
Linda	We'd only just started . . .
Question	What just at weekends?
Brian	When we got us giro or whatever. But like it were when that friend . . . when he brought that henry, that's what did it . . .
Linda	Yeh it just came into us life like and stayed . . .
Brian	I'll curse that bastard till't day I die, me, you know . . . But it were us own fault for saying yeh . . . It were just that henry made everything seem alreet . . .

Linda   But that was only for a while, though . . . two weeks probably.

Brian   Two weeks at most. And after that you wish you'd never seen the bloody stuff.

This timescale was undoubtedly something of an exaggeration, however, serving perhaps as a means by which Linda and Brian could express their self-disgust at having got involved with heroin in this almost haphazard way. Because at first, they only used heroin in the same way that they had used amphetamine on an occasional basis, and the frequency of their use only edged upwards slowly, suggesting that something more than two weeks were involved:

Linda At first it were only once a week.

Brian Yeh.

Linda Like we had that, then that were it weren't it? We didn't touch nowt else. And then again't week after . . .

Brian Yeh, like it used to be every Tuesday, or something like that . . . when't giro came . . .

Linda But like, even that gets to be an habit . . . like you don't know, we didn't know . . . having it every week.

Brian You don't realize it, but it does.

Linda And then it just . . . became more and more, then . . .

Brian Yeh. Twice a week, three times a week, then it got to every day like. And then . . .

Linda It gets to your head first, psychologically, it gets your head first before it's physical.

Brian Cos, it were't needle at first that got us, like we were a bit up-tight on't needle . . .

Linda Yeh, cos it's like two different addictions, you know . . .

Brian You're not addicted to it physically . . . you need it, like, but it's in your head . . .

How heroin comes to be a central feature of people's lives is also a question of how it begins to encircle their wider groups of friends and acquaintances. Linda and Brian described, for example, how after they had first started using heroin they had managed to obtain a new house. And this not only removed them from their former squalor, with which they associated the original attractions of heroin as a means of escape. By moving to the other side of town, they also hoped this would enable them to make a clean break from the drug. But it was not to be like that.

Linda Cos we thought when we moved down here we'd . . .
Brian . . . We'd get away from it.
Linda When we got this house, that were it, we thought . . .
Brian We thought, 'Oh we've done it here', we've cracked it like.
Linda But it didn't, it like followed us . . .
Brian It did, like we saw it spread . . . spreading all around't town through every area. Like we moved here at same time as they did [some friends] down't road. And like, we were doing henry then, like, when we moved in here . . . and they moved in down't road and they were doing henry then too.
Linda Cos people who are using it, just get in different places, you know . . . and it's there then isn't it?
Brian Yeh, it were like a black cloud weren't it, just kind of seeping over here . . .
Linda Yeh, it just came over.

It was probably about this time that heroin use arrived at a critical point in terms of its epidemic spread in their community, and it is an important observation that such a development might sometimes be associated with existing users changing their place of residence for whatever reason, thereby making it more likely that the drug will become available in different localities so that it penetrates into a wider number of friendship networks. This is not a question of people moving house deliberately in order to try to spread the drug around; rather, it is a consequence of people who are often in only a marginal position within the housing market (as Linda and Brian were), whose residence will therefore tend to be unsettled.

Brian People move into different places like, and . . . they start up when they get into that place . . . and others

get addicted like. I've seen people who'd said, 'Oh
no, I'll never touch it' . . . then, two months later,
he'd be going, 'Do you know where there's any
henry, man?' like . . . and you'd think, Fuck . . .
Wow, you just couldn't believe it. People who'd
never, ever . . . People who'd said, 'I'll not touch that
stuff', and you could see 'em like . . . 'Oh alright, I'll
just have a little dragon' . . .

Linda I mean, they should know better, you know what I
mean.

Brian When they'd seen us, like we'd tell 'em, 'Don't ever
do it man.'

Linda But we . . . we didn't see nobody when we were
starting, do you know?

Brian We didn't know anybody.

Linda No. We didn't know nobody . . . there were loads of
people using, like, but we weren't in that circle.

Brian We didn't associated wi' them. We were away from
it . . .

Linda . . . So you'd think people who saw you wouldn't,
but they did. You know, it overtook 'em anyway . . .
Like if we'd seen somebody, somebody turkeying . . .

Brian Aye, it would've put us off definitely.

Whether or not it would actually have deterred them, of
course, is another matter. Nevertheless, this is how they saw
it. The pattern of heroin use which Linda and Brian established
was in fact rather unusual. When they had first encountered
heroin, although there was a small but growing heroin
network in their home town, they were not associated with it
and their initial supply had come through a friend from
another locality where heroin was at that time more freely
available. Moreover, this distribution network was quite
separate from the one which operated in their home town,
which all meant that they started using heroin without having
any significant contact with other heroin users. And even
when they began to get more heavily involved with the drug,
they were still not at first in regular contact with the drug
culture of their immediate locality. So that when their supply

from out of town was suddenly interrupted, they were left high and dry:

Brian We were doing it for six month us, before't supply got cut . . . We were doing it for six months and we never turkeyed once in that six months . . . .

Linda Cos like where we getting it from were continuous, all't time.

Brian Until one day like, we went up to this place . . . and it were winter. It'd been snowing and it were coming from Manchester at that time, o'er t'Pennines . . . and there were a reet big downfall o' snow, and this guy got stuck in Manchester, couldn't get through. So it all dried up like. And we were . . . that neet, oh it were terrible weren't it?

Linda Yeh, we still didn't know what a turkey were then, cos we didn't associate with people who were . . . you know, they weren't our type of people like.

Brian Yeh we didn't know what it were, like . . . We just thought it were like dope.

Linda . . . and then we turkeyed and that, but from that day on . . .

Brian It were only six months like we'd been on it, and from that day . . . .

Linda We were hitting it hard for six months, and after . . .

Brian . . . for't next eighteen months, only when we had to . . .

This did not mean that they immediately stopped using heroin when they discovered that they were suffering from withdrawal symptoms, but Linda and Brian did nevertheless begin what proved to be a long, drawn out process of trying to get treatment in the form of methadone maintenance. And in the meantime, the pattern of their use became that they would buy as much heroin as they could afford when their fortnightly social security cheque came through, and eke that out as best they could.

Brian A gram were costing about £60 then . . .

Linda Yeh, but we couldn't get a gram all't time could we?

Brian	Oh no, only . . .
Linda	Like, all we had to go on it were us giro . . .
Brian	Yeh, all't lot . . . and when we didn't have it, we just turkeyed, but it were bad weren't it?
Linda	Cos that were only £80, giro like, and there were twenty quid then [laughs] to live on for a fortnight, plus family allowance you know . . .
Question	So what did you do when you ran out of money?
Linda	We were poorly.
Brian	Yeh, we laid out on't floor and waited while sommat happened. You'll always find it, like, you don't have to steal or owt, it still comes to you . . . Don't it? You don't have to steal, rob, or . . .

By this time, since their original supply had been cut off, Linda and Brian had become more integrated within the local heroin-using community. And within this community, in spite of the constant denials of friendship that one hears from ex-users, there is a friendship of sorts. Through which people will sometimes help each other through the rough patches, offering a fellow user a 'taste' of heroin to smooth over their withdrawal symptoms:

Linda	You see if somebody comes to your house, 'Oh can I hit this up? I'll give you a bit' . . . you say, 'Yeh, oh yeh' . . .
Brian	When you're turkeying, you're not going to refuse are you?
Linda	Even a little filter or something, it'll tek what you want off.
Brian	Take your turkey off like, but it'll still keep you on henry . . . You know we turkeyed a lot, us . . . really. That's what . . . we got sick of it in't end. Really sick of it. But doctor wouldn't have nowt to do wi' us, for months like.

This grim struggle, which lasted for something like eighteen months, until they were finally able to secure a prescription for methadone, is in sharp contrast to the 'high life' described by those who claimed to have been 'blasting' half a gram or more of heroin a day, and supporting their habits by various means of hustling or robbing. Linda and Brian did not turn to crime in order to support their habit, preferring instead to suffer withdrawal through the lean patches, thereby managing to retain a significant amount of self-respect. They also expressed considerable pride in the fact that, whatever difficulties they had to face, they had never allowed these to come between them. Indeed, they found that they had a vital resource in each other, so that when the going got really rough they were able to turn the corner and start the long climb back.

Brian I just says to her, I remember one day, I said: 'Look we've had it, us' . . . I says, 'we're here for ever.'
Linda Never gonna get off it.
Brian And then, like, she goes, 'Oh I'll bloody show you.' And then she never had a fix since . . .

As Linda understood it, what had rescued them was love:

Linda There's only one thing that gets yer off it, and that's love.
Brian Yeh.
Linda Honestly, there's nothing else.
Brian You've got to love somebody.

This was not really a happy ending, however, because there was still an awful lot of work to do. Even so, for Linda and Brian, friendship had not quite fallen apart.

The First Withdrawal: Two Women

When the first withdrawal symptoms appear, signalling the onset of a physical dependence on the drug, a heroin user is no longer in the 'grey area' and there is no longer any question of misinterpreting their degree of involvement with heroin. Now if heroin is not taken in sufficient quantity and with sufficient regularity, the user will suffer the displeasurable symptoms of a 'turkey' – running nose, high temperature, aches and pains, sleeplessness, sweating, sometimes diarrhoea and vomiting, and a restless discomfort together with a craving for the drug – until heroin is taken again or, after a few days of this discomfort, withdrawal runs its course and the symptoms cease. Heroin is no longer something to be taken for a 'hit' or a 'buzz'; it has become a 'habit' which must be sustained if the user is to stay 'normal' or 'straight'. It is always possible of course, as with a number of people that we have already met, that if someone had been using heroin for some time on a daily basis without giving themselves a chance to 'turkey', then they were already addicted long before they experienced their first withdrawal. But with the onset of the first withdrawal symptoms, their addicted status is now beyond question. Indeed, it is only when these symptoms first appear that someone can know for certain that they have become addicted.

For some people, withdrawal sickness is merely a confirmation of what they might have already feared or suspected. Even so, as it is often remembered, the first withdrawal appeared

quite unexpectedly. These were people who had not imagined
they would get 'hooked'. That was presumably something
which happened to other people.

But when it does happen to you, and not to other people,
how does it come about and what does it mean? We can
contrast the accounts of two women from different parts of the
north of England whose initial experiences with heroin were
utterly different, but who were both eventually taken by
surprise when they discovered that they suffered withdrawal
symptoms if they did not use heroin daily. Indeed, their
surprise was so total that neither of them realized what these
symptoms were when they first appeared.

Sharon: 'There was none of these adverts . . .'

Sharon is 21 years old, and she lives in one of the most
depressed regions of the country, in Merseyside, and she has
only been able to find work intermittently since she left school.
Sharon first used heroin four years ago when she was
seventeen years old. Prior to that she had smoked cannabis
occasionally, and she had also taken 'speed' a few times. But
she was not very experienced in drug affairs, and when she
first tried heroin it was only just beginning to appear in her
locality and there was no established heroin network, nor
much local knowledge of the drug's effects. In fact, when
Sharon and her girlfriend were first offered heroin by a friend,
they did not even know what it was:

'When we first started taking smack there was none of these
adverts or nothing like that, and it wasn't called heroin, it
was called "smack" . . . and it still is, like, but before it really
started getting as it is now, it was just called smack. And a
lad that we knew says to us, "Do you want some smack?"
And we said [in a whisper] "What's that?" He says, "It's a
substitute for heroin", or something, I can't really remember.
And he said, "You can't get hooked on it" and that like. So
we said, "Alright then", and me and a friend had a bag
between us. Well, we only had half the bag and we were

wrecked . . . really stoned. We thought, "It's alright this". So we just went on for about two weeks solid, just buying bags, and we'd smoke that like, and I didn't know what day it was or nothing . . . we must have done a terrible lot, and we were smoking a bag each then. And it just started getting that way, like, you need more to get the same hit. It's not like draw [cannabis] or anything like that. And then you end up taking it just to feel . . . normal, you know what I mean? Anyway, then after a solid month we started withdrawing. But when you first take smack and you're first withdrawing, you don't know what it is. Because, like as far as anyone knew you couldn't turkey off it. And I was just coming down with the shakes and all that, oh it was horrible. I thought I had the flu. And it wasn't until someone said to me, like, "Oh you're withdrawing" . . . I nearly died of shame.'

Whether or not it would have made any difference to Sharon's story if there had been a national advertising campaign (or local knowledge) to warn of heroin's dangers is of course highly questionable. We have already met too many people whose experience suggests otherwise. And it is all the more questionable in view of the fact that in 1981, when she first tried heroin, there was a sudden and dramatic alteration in the availability of the drug in the area where she lived. As she recalled it, the extent of heroin use among young people in her locality, where the drug had previously been quite unknown, underwent a quantum leap:

'You'd go round and everyone was just into draw. And then like, when we were taking smack, just first getting into it, there was a bit of it around, not much though. And then all of a sudden, everyone you met like, they'd go, "Such and such a person's a smackhead now" . . . "God, is he?" . . . "Yeh". It just went round, like it just seemed to get off in about two months. Everyone was on it. People I went to school with, who were really stuck up at school and that like, they were on it. It was just amazing, the people who were at it . . . It just come in all at once. It was hardly ever heard of was it? It's really been in the last two years, something like that . . . There's that much demand for it now. I don't know how they'll stop it, though. Not unless they do something drastic because there's that many people in demand for it.'

Sharon is speaking here of a locality in which a heroin problem of truly epidemic proportions has established itself within the past few years, and which has penetrated deeply into local youth cultures. In the neighbourhood in which she lived, unemployment was running at 35 per cent in 1981 when heroin first put in an appearance, and among young people under twenty-five years of age the unemployment rate touched 60 per cent. Subsequently, of course, as the economic recession has deepened this situation can only have got worse. Experience suggests that where heroin becomes available under such circumstances, it can move rapidly through a neighbourhood. Sharon was certainly not alone in her fate.

New forms of friendship and relationship were quickly established within Sharon's social orbit. She struck up with a boyfriend who tried his hand at small-scale dealing for a while, until he was caught and sent to prison. She used heroin regularly for four years, smoking up to a gram a day at times, with only occasional interruptions during times of scarcity which are a recurrent feature of the illicit heroin market. When there was 'drought' in the heroin market, she renewed her acquaintance with withdrawal sickness. Although her view of what withdrawal amounted to was somewhat ambiguous:

'Did you withdraw a lot?'

'Say . . . about four times badly since I've been on it. About four times really bad, that was for two days . . . I had the money as well, but there was a drought on . . . you couldn't get none anywhere. All that was going was grams, they're normally £60 . . . and they were going for £150 and that, a gram . . . people just rocketed it up and that like. The price goes like that when there's a drought on, but then it comes back down again.'

'What was it like, withdrawal?'

'As soon as you wake up, it's like a ton of bricks coming down on you like, "Where am I going to get my money from today?" But, like when you think about it now, most of it is psychological . . . Like you wake up and you think, "I should be turkeying" and that, but you're not turkeying . . . "What's going on? I'm not turkeying" . . . I think a lot of it's in your head . . . but I wouldn't say it was easy . . .'

In order to sustain her heroin habit Sharon began shoplifting and other forms of thieving, until she was eventually caught whereupon she entered treatment at the local clinic. She is now receiving a prescription for methadone on a maintenance basis. Some young women whom she knew had turned to prostitution in order to support their habits, although for Sharon heroin was now an episode in her life that hopefully had closed:

'It's my last warning that, going to court, I'll not risk it again like . . . but I've got my methadone now and that's it. It keeps you on the level, like, the methadone. But there's a lot still on it round here. In fact, I think there are more girls on it now than there is fellas really, you know, when you look around . . . I mean, if you went down there now where they hang around, it'd be all fellas. But, well all the girls are on the game, like so you don't see them until the night time . . . there's loads, all my mates are on it, on the game and that. So . . . that's it . . . [laughs] . . . that's my story.'

There is not much more to say about Sharon's heroin addiction. She had slipped into it in her late teens, without any real knowledge of the drug that she was using, at a time when getting a 'buzz' off heroin was rapidly becoming fashionable among other young people in her locality. She is no doubt the kind of young woman who is usually thought of as a victim of the heroin scene. And perhaps she is, although this is not the way that she would describe it:

'Why did you get into it, do you think? What's so good about heroin?'
  'At first you mean?'
  'Mm.'
  'The hit you get off it I think . . . Your first one, like it's just too much, you're just like walking on air. You feel really

good. And you get like that . . . say, for a couple of months, you know you can really get a hit off it and that like. And then before you know you're just addicted to it, so there's nothing you can do. It's just, like, one of them drugs that you get into . . . I'm not complaining, or anything like that. It gives you a buzz for the first couple of months, and then you really pay for it like. It is hard to get off it . . .'

Josephine: 'I hated it . . . I just slipped into it'

In sharp contrast, we can compare the experience of Josephine, from another part of the north of England to the east of the Pennines where heroin use is much less widespread. Josephine was an older woman who first began using heroin two years ago when she was already twenty-six years of age, and who had to overcome a great deal of initial reluctance before she would try the drug.

Josephine had worked as a nursery nurse with handicapped children for some years, a job which she enjoyed and which gave her enough money and free time to go out with friends at the weekend to clubs and parties. Unlike Sharon, she already had an extensive knowledge of the drugs scene which reached back to her late teens, and though she had enjoyable recollections of smoking cannabis she had also seen something of the unpleasant side of illicit drug use:

'We kept it in its right place then. All we did was have a smoke, you know smoke cannabis and that was all . . . It was just a social thing, it wasn't an important thing . . . Just a pound deal now and again and that was it . . . But there was a lot of acid about at the time, LSD, when I was about eighteen I think. I once had a tab of acid which I really enjoyed, it was really nice. But at the same time I saw a lot of people who . . . well, a couple of people who were quite close to me . . . it just totally freaked them out, acid you know. And I saw people deteriorate. One chap ended up in a mental hospital. His personality totally changed, and I just went, "I'll never take that again." It was freely available, but I just wasn't interested in that sort of psychedelic thing . . .'

A few years later she extended her involvement with illicit drugs, getting into the habit of 'snorting' a line of speed at the weekend with friends before going out for a night on the town. It was a period of her life that she looked back to with some fondness:

'It was tablets at first, "blueys", we used to call them "French blueys", and then amphetamine sulphate . . . but I wouldn't say I had a habit with speed or anything, I just sort of took it again as a social thing.'

'When did you take it?'

'Just whenever someone turned up with it really, you know, I mean to me it was a new thing that kept you awake and you were up all night, it was really good . . . You know, I enjoyed it, having a real good time. I used to go out . . . like to pubs and clubs. There was a club that we used all the time . . . We'd go to the pub; come back from the pub and have a line of speed, go to the club, dancing and that; then . . . we'd leave the club and have a card school or something at somebody's house, staying up all night and things like that. It was good.'

'Were any of the people you knew then using heroin?'

'No, there was no heroin. I'd never seen heroin until, what, about two years ago.'

Josephine's first encounter with heroin was when she went to stay with some friends of her boyfriend in another city, and it did not impress her at all:

'I can remember going there. We used to go and see these people and spend a weekend at their house. And we always went out, you know, to pubs and clubs and whatever. As I say, I was that kind of person, I loved going out a lot. But, we hadn't seen them for a while, and they'd got into heroin, and I went there with my boyfriend for a weekend, and I just couldn't . . . I just packed my bags and left after sort of a day and half. Because they were all just sitting around, you know not doing anything, didn't want to go to the pub, didn't want to go out. And I just couldn't understand it . . . I wanted to go out, you know I wanted to go to the pubs, I wanted to go out shopping during the day and things like that. And they just weren't interested any more . . .'

Things were to take a dramatic turn in Josephine's life, however, when her boyfriend who worked in manufacturing industry was made redundant. He was a skilled mechanic, but there were no jobs available and he hated going down to the Job Centre because of all the gloomy people who hung around there. He became depressed and started using 'speed' more often, and not only at weekends. He also began mixing with a new crowd, some of whom were using heroin; it must have been around this time that he first tried heroin himself and found that he enjoyed it. He often rolled in at all hours of the night and early morning during the week, and he had no trouble financing his 'high life' because he had not only a lot of spare time on his hands, but also a substantial amount of redundancy pay. Josephine eventually became tired of this and decided to give up her own job for a short time, partly to see if she could help her boyfriend to sort himself out, and partly to join in the high life. But from what she had to say, she clearly still did not approve of her boyfriend's new friends or their lifestyle:

'He met up with a lot of people, and they started coming to my house and they were all using heroin, and I used to go mad . . . I didn't like them in the house, you know, I wouldn't let people in the house if they injected. It's not that I wouldn't let them inject in the house, I just wouldn't let them in the house, full stop, if I knew that they used the needle. They just didn't come into my house and that was it. I used to go mad, you know.'

So, how then had she got involved with heroin herself, given her hostility to what she had seen of heroin and its incompatibility with her accustomed lifestyle? To this day she remains puzzled as to how she developed a heroin habit herself:

'I didn't think I would ever have got involved. I mean, I hated it. And I hated them too. And then when I did use it, how I got a habit I don't know, because for months it made me so ill . . . The first time I tried smack, it just made me

violently sick. But then . . . I just kept taking it.'
  'But why?'
  'I don't know, I just can't understand it myself. I suppose
it was because it was there . . . You see, I didn't think I had
any problems with it because I didn't have to pay for it.
Because my boyfriend's friends were all using it and that,
giving it to me . . . They were always offering me chases and
at first I was refusing it, but in the end I just gradually
slipped into it. And then, as I say, one day I sort of realised
that I'd had it every day for six days.'

By chance, it was just at this time that Josephine had
arranged to visit a friend in a distant town. And although she
had now been taking heroin regularly, it did not occur to her to
take any with her on this trip – partly because the friend she
was to visit was not interested in drugs, but also because it
never occurred to her that she might be addicted.

She was away for three days, and Josephine noticed that she
did not feel too well, although again it did not occur to her that
this might have anything to do with heroin. 'I just didn't feel
myself', she said, 'wound up, agitated, I just didn't feel well.'
In fact, she had had a row with the friend whom she had gone
to visit, which had upset her, and had wondered whether this
was what the trouble might have been. On her return journey
home she began to feel poorly again, including what she
described as a 'craving'. But still she did not make any
connection between these symptoms of distress and her heroin
use. It was only when she had a 'chase' with some friends
when she got home, whereupon her symptoms disappeared,
that she realized what had happened:

  'When you say you felt terrible, what did you feel like?'
  'Oh just absolutely useless . . . I had this craving as well.
As I say I'd had it for six days constantly before I went away
for a few days. But all the time I was away I just didn't
feel . . . right . . . you know, I just didn't feel myself. I
felt . . . wound up, agitated, and I just didn't feel well.'
  'And you knew if you had some heroin it would bring you
back to normal?'
  'Oh no. I didn't know. I didn't know that. In fact when I

went round to those friends, I didn't go deliberately to get some heroin . . . In fact I think I went round to borrow a bottle of milk. You see I'd just got back and there was nothing in the house.'

She may not have know then, but she knew now, and Josephine began to use heroin on a daily basis from that day onwards: 'It just progressed from there', she said.

Varieties of experience: a great leveller

Neither Sharon nor Josephine realised that they had developed an addictive pattern of heroin use until the first withdrawal symptoms appeared, and even then they had not initially recognized that it was withdrawal they were suffering from. But in other respects their experiences of heroin in the 'grey area' of transitional use had been quite different. Sharon had first tried the drug in the company of a girlfriend who was also novice, and they had immediately enjoyed the 'buzz': it was like 'walking on air', she said. For Josephine, her initial encounters with heroin had been within a circle of experienced users whom she had actively disliked, and nor did she immediately take to the drug which for some time made her violently ill. And whereas when Sharon had first accepted heroin she had been quite ignorant of what it was, Josephine had been reluctant to try a drug that was used by people whom she judged to be utterly despicable. Sharon also had to pay for the drug almost from the beginning, buying £5 bags with her friend; for Josephine heroin was freely on tap within her circle of friends and acquaintances.

There were also fundamental differences in terms of the areas in which they lived, and the lifestyles that were associated with heroin use. Sharon began using heroin at a time when the habit was spreading rapidly among young people in her locality, where it was at first associated with a novel kind of risk and excitement. Josephine, on the other hand, lived in an area where the heroin network tended to involve older people, and where it was also much smaller and less obtrusive, having settled down into its recluse and inward-looking routines of staying at home and doing little else. Finally, there was the question of age and experience. Sharon was not yet eighteen years old when she first tried heroin, having accepted 'smack' on the first occasion that it was offered to her. Whereas Josephine was already in her late twenties, with a respectable job, and she had persistently refused offers of 'chases' for some months before she finally accepted. But for all these initial differences, their subsequent experiences were very similar, involving a rapid and imperceptible drift as they crossed the threshold of transitional use into addiction. Heroin, in this sense, can be a great leveller.

Three Friends:
Alternative Routes and Choices

The impression that is so often given in these accounts of a person's early experimentation with heroin and their transition through the 'grey area' into addiction is one of an inevitable and relentless process. 'It becomes part of your body' is how Boy George put it in a television interview after his own problems with heroin had become public knowledge:

'I thought I could control it, which is what every intelligent person thinks. But with heroin it isn't like that. You can't handle it. You don't have any choice or control. It is the boss.' (*London Standard*, 6 August 1986)

In retrospect, the transition into addiction is so often remembered as if it had been simply inevitable. But the 'grey area' of transitional use does not necessarily take this form, and some people can and do arrest their involvement with the drug and avoid what will otherwise be the inevitable consequence of daily heroin use. Taking Josephine's phrase, 'I gradually slipped into it', for example, it is reasonable to suppose that over a period of weeks and months certain conscious choices and decisions were made. And also that these decisions would sometimes involve various kinds of subterfuge, whereby people hide from themselves the obvious consequences of their actions.

Perhaps the most common form which these subterfuges take is revealed in the often repeated expression, 'One little toot won't do me any harm': a self-deception whereby someone says to themselves that they will do it again today, but not tomorrow. And then when tomorrow comes around, the same act of bad faith: 'Just one more little toot . . .'; 'Just one more little chase . . .'

One of the characteristics of accounts often given by heroin users and ex-users is that they rarely embrace any recognition of their own motivation and agency. So that the drift into addiction is remembered only as something in which one played a passive role – as if the user were powerless in the face of a relentless pharmacological process, and later driven by the overriding concern to avoid the symptoms of withdrawal. But there is something highly dubious about accounts such as these. What one needs to ask, in a preliminary way, is: what is it that is so overpowering and frightening about withdrawal symptoms which Sharon first mistook for a dose of the flu, and which Josphine endured for three days without realising that they had anything to do with heroin at all?

The various choices and options which people will face in the early stages of their heroin use, and which will determine whether or not they will continue to use the drug, will depend on a number of factors. The initial experience can sometimes be a violent sickness which can itself deter someone from further experimentation – though this cannot be relied upon as an effective deterrent, as numerous accounts have shown. On the other hand, someone might find that the effects of heroin are too overpowering to enable them to continue with their accustomed lifestyle, in which case the drug will hold few attractions. The local availability of drugs and shifting patterns of drug preference within local drug cultures are also vital influences on people's drug choices. Or, it might simply be a question of friendship once more. Someone who has begun to use heroin might simply lose contact with the group of people with whom they were mixing, in which case their access to the drug could dry up at an early stage of their experimentation. Or, it might be that they break up with a boyfriend or girlfriend. Friendship, as we have come to see, is invariably decisive.

Three friends, three different choices:
'I weren't that bothered . . .'

It would be wrong to think of these contexts of friendship as only concerning 'bad company' which can lead people astray. Friendship can be both the route into certain kinds of drug choices, and also the way out. And even within a single friendship network, different people will nevertheless exercise different options and at different times, in such a way that the outcomes of their heroin experiences will significantly differ.

Take, for example, three young people who lived in a part of Yorkshire with a substantial heroin problem, who all came into contact with heroin, and yet for whom the outcomes were quite different. Cheryl is twenty years old, and she had developed what in her own words was a 'greedy' heroin habit which she had maintained, largely by shoplifting, for nearly two years. Her brother Wayne, who was one year older, had also mixed in the local drug culture, although with a different outcome, as he found that he didn't like opiates at all. Morphine, when he first tried it, simply made him ill. Wayne's girlfriend, Wendy, on the other hand, who was also twenty-one years old and a close friend of Cheryl's, had got into heroin quite seriously – until she quit rather abruptly. So that, whereas Cheryl now received a prescription for methadone linctus, Wendy no longer used opiates at all.

In the beginning, the experiences of both Cheryl and Wendy had been very similar. As Cheryl explained:

'I were reet dead against it, weren't I, cos I'd had this friend what used to be into it, and I'd seen how she were and that, and I hated it didn't I? And then, when I started living wi' this bloke what were dealing a bit, when I started living wi' him I started on it . . . only smoking it, you know "dragoning", I never fixed for ages. And then I started fixing . . .'

This was a locality where injecting seemed to be almost as common as smoking, and where illicit pharmaceuticals were also as commonly available as imported 'brown' heroin.

Wendy, who had first got into heroin before she knew either Cheryl or Wayne, again described how the early stages of her heroin use had followed an entirely familiar pattern. She had also been living with a young man who was using heroin heavily, and who had since gone to prison:

Wendy   When I got into it, I had no choice like but to get into it really. Cos like I were living wi' this lad, and . . . no money like. Not eating or nowt. No food in't house. And all there were, were smack, all't time. And I always used to refuse it, and then once I said yeh. Y'know, I used to have . . . look forward to it then, y'know, cos there were nowt else. You know, I never used to move out of't house like.

Question And were you sick, the first time you . . .

Wendy   Oh aye . . . [as if this had been a silly question] . . . Y'always are . . .

Cheryl   After a bit, like, I got used to it me, I were having loads . . .

Wendy   You look forward to it, don't you? You know, taste . . . that taste in yer mouth. You look forward to it in't end don't you . . . you know, that taste what makes you . . . [gestures] . . . find a toilet quick. Well like, in't end . . .

Cheryl   Yeh, it's nice.

Wendy began to smoke heroin regularly, although unlike Cheryl she never really liked the idea of injecting. She preferred 'chasing' or 'dragoning'. But then after six months of solid use she stopped. Why?

Question Wendy, how did you manage to keep it under control then, do you think?

Wendy   Well, I didn't get much money. I used to shoplift, but I were scared o' doing't shoplifting, scared o' getting caught. And that stopped me from using. I think if I could've had more I would've done.

Cheryl   Yeh, you do, don't you.

Wendy   But like, I never had any money, and no way o' getting it . . . I wouldn't risk me liberty like.

Wayne	She were knocking abaht wi' people that were into it, that's how she . . .
Wendy	At one time like, for about six month I were using it,.y'know, pretty regularly but . . . I weren't ever *that* bothered anyway. I liked buzz I got, but . . . I weren't bothered about being an addict. You know what I mean. I didn't want to go that far like.

In this part of Yorkshire, as with the Lancashire dialect in some areas, to say that you are 'not bothered' about something does not necessarily mean that you do not care. It can also mean that you are not particularly interested in something. So that when Wendy says, 'I weren't bothered about being an addict', it does not mean that she was unconcerned about the likelihood that she might become an addict, but that the addict lifestyle did not interest or attract her. Why, then, did she give up heroin? Was it because she had split up with her former boyfriend?

Wendy	No. You see, I were knocking about wi' him, and he got sent down, and then I were knocking about wi' this lass . . . and that's when I were really into it like . . . But like, I were knocking about wi' her, and lifting wi' her, you know, I got into lifting . . . and then I got caught again and I were scared. Stopped lifting, and then I . . . you know . . . didn't use as much then. And then I met Wayne, and then I didn't use anything . . . so . . .

She liked the 'buzz' that she got off heroin, but that was all. The fear of getting caught for shoplifting outweighed the attractions of the drug, so that at first she began to use heroin less frequently to match her economic means, and then stopped altogether.

At this point Wayne chipped in with his own experience, which was different again:

Wayne	First bad thing I ever had were morphine, like. And that were't first time I'd ever touched a drug
Question	What, did you sniff that?
Cheryl	No, injected.

Wayne	Were it morphine?
Cheryl	Morphine, yeh.
Wayne	And it were fixed on me, like, that were't first . . .
Cheryl	Rush knocked 'im aht!
Wayne	And there were no way I were gonna touch owt after that, like.
Question	You didn't like it, then, did you?
Cheryl	*I've* O-D'd!
Wayne	I'd seen everybody do it, and I wanted to try it. And like, I hated it after that. That were't first and last, like, know what I mean . . . no chance.
Mother	But you're one o' them, what if yer gets a reet 'ard knock, or . . . if that falls tha faints! Thy ought to 'ave known having't needle . . .
Wayne	But like, I just wanted to try it . . . but effect it had on me like, I just thought scrub that. You know what I mean, no chance.

After this unpleasant experience, Wayne has never been tempted to try opiates again. Even so, he remained loyal to his sister Cheryl and helped her to sustain her own habit, running around to score for her if she was not feeling well enough. Cheryl's own account of her experiences with heroin was in sharp contrast to those of both Wayne and Wendy, in that she had maintained her habit for something like two years with great determination through shoplifting, until she was eventually caught too many times. Her conversational style was also rather different, in that she tended to dwell upon gruesome details of drug overdoses which she had survived, together with reminiscences of 'turkeying' and pharmacological feats-of-strength involving the prodigious quantities of heroin that she had consumed. But then, she had been much more heavily involved:

Cheryl	I think lasses are more greedier than lads, honest I do. I were reet greedy, me. I were knocking about wi' this lad, Martin, and we'd just had a fix and I'd say, I haven't got nowt off that and have another one. And I had really . . . just reet greedy.
Mother	I think lasses . . . er . . . it's 'arder for lasses to come

off it, in't it and all? I don't think lasses 'ave got will-
power as strong as men . . .

Cheryl I were spending hundred-and-odd quid a day on it,
me, gooin' out shoplifting to get . . . y'know I
wouldn't come home until I had hundred-and-odd
quid for my smack. I've known missen, me and this
kid, have earned two-hundred-and-odd quid wi'
shoplifting and it's all gone on it. As much money as
I've had, I've spent it all on smack. More money I've
had, more smack I've had . . .

It was characteristic of her mother's response that she should
refer to a lack of 'will-power' as a reason for Cheryl's and other
people's heroin misuse. Cheryl's great determination in
pursuing 'smack', however, suggests a strength of purpose of
its own, although it did also involve considerable self-neglect.
At one point, her body-weight dipped as low as six stones as
she began to disregard everything other than heroin and its
associated lifestyle. Cheryl was nevertheless careful to point
out that she had 'never gone as low' as to steal from her
mother or friends. But she was increasingly only mixing with
other heroin users, injecting and sharing needles, and putting
the patience of her family and remaining friends to a severe
test:

Cheryl I used to be reet gobby and bitchy, didn't I? Nobody
could say nowt to me.
Wayne She used to be full of spots as well . . .
Wendy She were one o't worst, her.
Mother I think they lose a lot of friends and all, heroin
addicts.
Cheryl Oh I did, aye. My school mates, if I seen 'em I didn't
want to know 'em . . . they were plastics cos they
didn't take smack. You know, everybody had to take
smack to be alreet . . .

Even when she overdosed, Cheryl did not remember being
at all deterred from her lifestyle:

Cheryl I once O-D'd on it, and I thought . . . about half a
gram o' smack, and I thought it were horrible. And I

died an' all . . . I did, I deed, honest . . . It never
put me off. It did for't rest o't day like, but . . . I
didn't know nowt.

Mother Tha wouldn't know, would thi', if tha'd O-D'd . . .
tha'd know nothin'. Tha'd have no feeling or nowt.

Cheryl I didn't know nowt . . . so it didn't put me off like.

Mother That's what I say . . .

In spite of all this difficulty and hazard, Cheryl's account of
this period of her life, when she was heavily involved in heroin
use, was sometimes almost gleeful, in that she could still revel
in her notoriety. Here, for example, she is describing a time
when she had moved back into her mother's house with a
friend who was also using heroin:

Cheryl We used to be reet obvious. Like, I'd get up in a
morning turkeying and I'd be reet quiet wouldn't I?
Reet bad tempered like . . .

Mother And if I said owt, she'd scream and shout.

Cheryl I'd go out . . . then come running in, like, skipping
and this . . . [gestures] . . . and she'd know. She'd
say, 'Thar's a lot happier since this morning.' And
like we'd go upstairs, soon as we come in, be
upstairs ages . . . We were reet obvious us, weren't
we? We never tried to hide it . . . I did like, but now
I think about it . . . not really did I? And you were
always coming in't bedroom catching me . . . and I
were always nicking spoons, and . . .

Wayne She were reet obvious. Always leaving shreds of
evidence around . . . black marks on't spoons and
that.

The extent of Wayne's involvement with his sister during
this heavy phase of her heroin use was not entirely clear. He
had never become involved in shoplifting with her, but in one
way or another he had helped her to maintain her habit, even
though his loyalties were sometimes stretched. Characteristi-
cally, Wayne put the problem down to the bad company
which Cheryl was keeping:

Wayne That's how I think it happens most o't time missen

[i.e. myself], wi't company sort of thing, y'know one thing leads to a bigger thing . . .

Cheryl　You've knocked abaht wi' me for a bit, though, haven't you? He, like, were running all ovver wi' me for it . . .

Wayne　I used to run . . .

Cheryl　All ovver didn't yer? God, [laughs] I've run 'im all ovver!

Wayne　I never used it.

Cheryl　Never touched it hissen.

Wayne　I've not used it missen . . .

Mother　A lot on 'em, a lot of heroin users, they don't realise what they do to their parents, definitely don't . . . Cos I have roared [i.e. cried], haven't I?

Wayne　That's one thing that were getting *me* mad, like. I were wi' Cheryl, like, and . . . ooh, she *were* using it. And I were running abaht wi' her . . . and then I've got my mother like, sort of asking questions. And I don't want to be saying owt about her, but I don't want to be lying to my mother. Do you know what I mean? And it were 'ard for me that were like.

While Cheryl continued to use heroin, Wayne remained loyal to his sister, sometimes protecting her from their mother's wrath; and it was only after she had begun to receive a methadone prescription that he became openly hostile to 'smack'. At first Cheryl sometimes used methadone excessively in order to 'gouch out' on it, although now after six months she was making slow if fitful progress to reduce her daily dosage. Cheryl was still a long way from relinquishing her dependence on opiates, but Wayne and Wendy tried to encourage her and to offer a positive image of her progress:

Cheryl　He [the psychiatrist] cuts you down gradually, you just get off it gradually, but . . . like, I can't remember, but I know I finished a day earlier . . . Oh he'd cut me down, that were it . . .

Wendy　Aye he'd cut you down, then he put you back onto't same level.

Wayne　She couldn't do it.

Cheryl   I couldn't do it, you know I couldn't manage wi' what he were geeing me.

Wendy   It weren't lasting you long enough were it?

Cheryl   So I finished a day earlier didn't I . . . and I were dying. Well, I weren't, but . . .

Wayne   But like since that, you've gone back haven't you, and you've told him that, like . . . She's gone back hersen and said, 'Cut me down a bit'. Haven't you?

Cheryl   Oh aye.

Wayne   Do you know what I mean, like, that's what you've got to be able to do, isn't it?

Wendy   Too much isn't good for you though, is it Cher?'

Cheryl   Oh no . . .

Wendy   You know if she's got too much she'll use more, waint you? Like . . . it doesn't do you good does it?

Cheryl   I . . . at first, when I first started getting it I were having it to get wiped out off it. Cos if you have enough you can get . . . you can get an hit off it like . . . Phhh, I looked terrible didn't I? Well, I were gouched.

Wendy   She only uses what she should do now.

Wayne   If she uses too much, we can tell straight away that . . .

Wendy   We *tell* her and all, don't we?

Wayne   Aye we tell her. But like, we can't really . . . we can't go on at her, you know what I mean. Because, like, she's got past stage o' using heroin hasn't she? And like she *is* helping hersen now. And I don't take it as same, you know tekking . . . medical stuff like linctus, or owt like that. I don't think it's same as heroin like.

Friendship holds together: 'I didn't kick you out . . .'

Even within a close group of friends, then, there can be quite opposed responses to the initial experiences of heroin use, and quite different outcomes. Wayne tried opiates only once, because he was curious about the effects, but that was all. He was at a party where some people were 'fixing' morphine, and in common with most novices where the injection-barrier is crossed, he had to have someone inject it for him ('It were fixed on me like'). The effect was immediate and unpleasant. 'First and last,' he said, 'scrub that.'

Wendy was initally frightened to try heroin, but she eventually accepted an offer from a boyfriend who she was living with, and then gave up after six months when she discovered that she did not have the temperament for shoplifting. 'I was never really *that* bothered,' she said about the effects of the drug. She liked the buzz, but that was it. Although there was still some remaining mystery about the extent of Wendy's actual involvement with heroin, which only began to be unravelled as the discussion developed. For a novice user who was 'never really that bothered' about heroin, she seemed to know far too much about the local drug scene, the people who participated in it and the various technologies of opiate use. Indeed, at one point she let drop that she had in fact injected herself. 'When I used to fix,' she said, grimacing, 'I used to go like that me . . . I couldn't look.' The fact that her involvement was actually deeper than she had initially implied, however, means that her cessation of heroin use was all that much more interesting.

Wendy   I think that were another thing that bothered me, t'parents finding out. I do. I'd a died, you know, if my mam and dad had've found out, y'know it would've reet hurt them, and they never . . . they know about that lad I were knocking around wi', but they never knew about me. They've always thought it, but they still today don't know, you know, that I've been into it . . . That's a good thing, really, isn't it? You know, that I packed it in before they found out . . .

Question   It's interesting that you managed to keep it under control.

Wendy   I used it for about six month, but not . . . I didn't get addicted.

Question   What, so you just used it at weekends then, or . . .

Wendy   I used it every day. But I were never . . . I weren't
           addicted to it . . .
Question   Perhaps it's a psychological thing or something? I
           don't know
Mother   I think it's something to do with . . . [inaudible,
           everyone talking at once] . . .
Wendy   It depends what you want to get out of it . . .
           When I met you Wayne, I were . . . I were . . .
           [inaudible] . . . somebody to get me away from all
           what . . . you know, from lifting every day. Like
           cos, I couldn't lift, and . . . I'd got to go down
           town and just walk around town for hours, you
           know, in't hope . . . that . . . I could nick summat
           for a bit o' smack . . .
Mother   But don't you think a lot of people are stronger . . .
Wendy   . . . so when I met him I were glad, you know, to
           just put it all behind me.

Most authorities would agree that at a purely physiological
level, after six months of daily heroin use someone would have
developed a physical dependence on the drug. But that was
not how Wendy saw it. She had other fish to fry, and refused
to embrace the idea that she had become an 'addict'. Whatever
complex motivations were at work (and mother's appeal to
'strong will-power' certainly fails to fit the bill) Wendy's
reluctance to find favour in the addict lifestyle, or to see any
value or worth in it for her, was perhaps a key issue in
enabling her to contain her identification with heroin even
when she was using it regularly. Then, when she met Wayne,
it clinched what she had already started and she has not used
heroin since that time. As our later discussion will show, many
users find that 'coming off' heroin is not all that difficult: it is
'staying off' that is the problem, and one way in which this
problem can be overcome is by a change in friendship patterns.
And Wendy's new boyfriend, Wayne, was quite an experienced hand – with a sister who revelled in the 'junkie' identity,
and his own first disastrously beneficial encounter with
morphine which had 'knocked him out'.
Cheryl, on the other hand, *liked* being knocked out.

Although it is important to recognize that her vivid accounts of 'gouching out' did not only reflect a remorseless pleasure in the prospect of obliteration, they also indicated something of the family's accustomed modes of interaction. Cheryl's account is in a large part a consequence of a role which she had been allotted within the family, a role through which she could claim attention and sympathy both within the family and also within the microcosm of the interview. Because Wayne and Wendy are success stories of a sort within this heroin narrative, and their claims on our attention are thereby much enhanced. Whereas Cheryl on the other hand, who was only halfway to a solution, was saying things that we have all heard so many times before. She was off heroin, and on methadone. Wayne struggled to make the most of this distinction, and to stress the positive side of this limited advance. Cheryl struggled, with only fitful success, to reduce the daily dose and to edge herself towards eventual withdrawal and abstinence.

Cheryl also had to struggle quite hard sometimes to make herself heard in the family. The family's own definition of itself, promoted particularly by mother but also by Wayne, was that it was a 'strong' family which had shown its strength by standing by Cheryl through thick and thin. But as we have seen, Wayne's brotherly loyalty – which was unquestionably strong and committed – had been somewhat ambiguous in that it had for some time involved helping Cheryl to maintain her habit, as well as helping her to deceive their mother.

At one point, Cheryl tried, but unsuccessfully, to make the interesting observation that it was not so much family support that helped her to discover the motivation to do something about her problem, but the threat that this support might be removed. This, however, could not be allowed, perhaps because it threatened the family perception of itself as a 'strong' family, capable of weathering any storm. Indeed, it caused the most unholy row which reduced Cheryl to tears:

Wayne But like, I think one o't reet essential things like, if you . . .
Mother Having a family to . . .
Wayne . . . If you want to get off on your own, you've got

to have a family or somebody behind you to stick by
you . . .

Mother . . . A family to stand by you.

Cheryl Ah, what really triggered me off is, my ma kicked
me aht . . . Didn't you? And it reet upset me that.

Mother I didn't kick you out.

Cheryl You did kick me aht.

Mother Now then . . .

Wayne Story were, there were two . . . she were living with
a friend at my mother's . . .

Cheryl God almighty mum . . .

Mother [Voice raised] We didn't kick yer out!

Wayne . . . And her and this friend, they were both using
heroin at me mam's . . . and . . .

Cheryl Well did you tell me to go or not?

Mother I says if you don't want to bide by my rules, that's
what I said to her . . .

Wayne . . . And they were both . . . they were both . . .

Mother [Voice raised] . . .If you don't want to bide by my
rules . . .

Cheryl I know . . . I were gonna say . . .

Wendy [Whispers to Cheryl] stop arguing . . .

Mother . . . Just put the key there and don't bother to come
back!

Cheryl . . . You weren't waiting for what I wanted to
say . . . [to Wendy] . . . was she though? . . . I were
going to say that she kicked me out, and . . .
[sobbing] . . . then that triggered it off, I knew I had
to get off it . . .

Even friends can fall out, and after they had patched up their
differences, they could laugh and joke together again about
some of the more absurd things that had happened in their
locality around the 'smack' scene. But there were also reasons
for regret: that everything had been much better before heroin
became available, when the only drug widely used was 'blow'
(cannabis), and people could go down town to a pub 'The
George', now a pub notorious for dealing, and have a good time.

Cheryl Ages ago, you know, when it were just blow . . .

you know, you could go in and sit wi' anybody, nobody'd pinch off you or nowt . . . you were all good mates.

Wendy We used to go there and dance, didn't we?

Mother And now, you have to go wi' everything in your pockets and no handbag!

Wayne It's powder, it's powder what's done it. You know what I mean? I think police accepted it, like, that the George were full o' blow, and like they never thought about a big bust or owt like that . . .

Cheryl They never really busted it. They've only busted it this time thinking there's smack, I'm telling you.

Wayne I mean people what've used it, and people what've been in theer, have abused it . . .

Wendy Oh aye . . . I remember dragoning in't tap-room . . .

Cheryl I've fixed in't toilets theer, me.

Mother Well, you can't blame 'em for busting it for that . . . Cos smack's harmful innit?

Wayne Well that's their job, isn't it? That's what I'm saying . . . Before it were respected like. There were blow in theer like, but leave 'em alone. Now they've got heavy on it, cos it's been abused. Know what I mean?

Making drug choices:
'Cos we do have discussion about it . . .'

The conversation drifted into a consideration of drugs more generally, with some mixed feelings as to whether legality was useful as a guiding principle on the harmfulness of different drugs. 'Look at folks smoking like chimneys,' said mother who smoked herself, 'and all them adverts – you still get all them adverts for fags, even though doctors say that's most harmful of all't lot!' The three friends were agreed that smoking cannabis was a harmless enough pursuit, although mother was not too sure.

Mother You see, I argue wi' these o'er blow. They say, 'Oh

it's nowt'. But it is . . . leads to bigger things . . . [chorus of protest] . . . I don't care. Yer've got to 'ave a strong mind for it *not* to lead to sommat bigger, haven't you? Whereas you've only got young minds . . .

Cheryl   Mother, as if I'm going to go back onto smack now anyway!

Mother   I've never said you are.

Cheryl   No, but way you said that . . .

Mother   I'm just saying, I've always argued . . .

Wayne   No, but look at us now.

Mother   Cos we do 'ave discussion abaht it, we do talk abaht it . . .

Wendy   We're reet now, aren't we?

Wayne   I mean, we 'avent't got young minds have we like. We've been through . . . a little bit haven't we, like . . . seen how, like . . .

And then later, when the discussion came back the same way, there was another question to consider. Where do you draw the line in a discussion of drug choices? Methadone was clearly a difficult area for this family. But what about alcohol, was that to be included? Was taking an aspirin part of the same pattern? What precisely should count as a 'drug'?

Wayne   I hate drugs and all like that now, you know like . . . I mean we just . . . I just wanted to get settled down in a place, and . . .I didn't want owt . . . no drugs, or . . . well, blow like. I still blow, you know what I mean . . .

Mother   I don't know what thee wants drugs into thee heads for, tekking 'em . . .

Wendy   We don't go out nowhere . . . We don't go out drinking, we just have a blow now and again don't we? No money like.

Wayne   We'd rather pay five pound . . .

Mother   Because I'm the big non-believer in tablets . . . I will *not* take a tablet . . .

Wayne   Well, we'd rather pay . . .

Mother   They could come round to my house and say, 'Have

you got a tablet for't headache', and I used to say, no . . . An headache'll go as it comes . . .

Wayne We'd rather pay . . .

Mother . . . I don't even take 'em, do I? Tek nothin' . . . [Wendy laughs that Wayne can't get a word in edgeways] . . . Not unless I'm forced. If I'm really ill, I will tek tablets, but . . .

Wayne We'd rather pay a fiver, like, to get . . . to feel alreet for a couple of nights . . .

Wendy A fiver gets three on us wiped out, donnit?

Wayne Against probably a tenner to go out supping.

Wendy A fiver doesn't last two minutes wi' me and you, does it? It's like . . .

Cheryl I hate drinking . . .

Wendy A pint and a half, it's over a quid. But if we get a fiver's worth o' blow . . . three of us get, or even if anybody else is here . . . we get stoned.

Mother But even that's illegal though isn't it?

Wayne I know it is but like . . .

Wendy It shouldn't be, though, blow . . .

Mother I mean, *I've* had blow.

Cheryl She does . . . listen to her! She puts it down, but she'll have it hersen!

Mother Oh aye? How often will *I* have blow?

Wendy I don't think blow should be illegal.

Mother How *often* will I have a blow?

Cheryl In Doncaster yesterday, or whenever I went, here listen to this! I went to Donny one day last week, and it said . . . on this big sign in't bus station, it said 'Cannabis Smokers Hate Heroin'!

Wayne Yeh, that's good that . . .

Wendy That's when't George were good, when it were just blow.

Mother [To the interviewer] But it is harmless isn't it, cannabis?

The only honest answer to that question – the one that was given – is that there are all manner of conflicting opinions held in expert circles about the health status of moderate cannabis use. It was probably not a question that was intended to provoke an answer, in any case. Drugs choices are shaped not merely by health education advice, but also by considerations such as what intoxicants are available and at what price. In an area of exceptionally high unemployment, the question of price in this instance was quite crucial. And still, of course, there are the binding contexts of friendship and kinship which help to fashion people's drug choices – friendship which in their young lives had already proved so powerful, first in drawing them into the world of heroin, and then enabling them to struggle out of it.

If their discussion of drug preferences seemed sometimes naive, then that is hardly surprising. Inhabiting, as we all do, a world in which drugs are a common currency – drinking, smoking, tablets for headaches, pills for colds – they had added to the repertoire a number of other permutations to juggle with. In the area in which they lived, a poor, run-down part of a northern industrial town blighted by the collapse of its industrial base, illicit drugs had become part of a 'way of life' for so many of their wider groups of friends and acquaintances. Not only heroin, which had brought Cheryl so low, but also other opiates, as well as cannabis, amphetamine sulphate, LSD and the rest. Then, there was the influence of the locally available treatment facilities for heroin addiction which were heavily reliant on the prescription of methadone, with some patients receiving injectable methadone in ampoule form: so that local medical practices themselves carried a barely hidden message that the way to deal with a problem with one drug was to substitute another. Who is then to say that having a 'blow' with friends from time to time was anything more than a cheap and harmless pastime, were it not for the fact that it is against the law?

In terms of how to exercise informed drug choices, they were quite literally having to make it up as they went along. 'It's queer isn't it,' said Wayne, 'when it were just blow, everyone were saying, "Got to be careful wi' that" like. But now since heroin's come along, people take blow as normal.' 'Is that speed addictive?' mother asked innocently; 'You know, what do they call it, sulphate . . . I don't think any o' them here's

been into that, but is that addictive?' 'Oh I hate speed', said
Cheryl: 'Whizz they call it now, I hate it.' 'It's powders again,
you see', said Wayne, 'it's all down to't powders.

Cheryl decided that it was getting late and that she had to go
out to get some food in before the shops closed. It was a sign
of the important changes in their lives that she remembered to
take her purse. As Cheryl busied herself to get ready, Wendy
suddenly asked another innocent question:

Wendy   Have you got to have some sort of O levels or A
        levels and that to start groups up, you know . . .
Mother You haven't got to have anything, all you've got to
        have is . . .
Wendy   We'd be alright wouldn't we like, us starting
        something?
Mother . . . Commonsense knowledge . . .
Wendy   You know, a group like . . .
Mother . . . Knowledge of what you're talking about.
Wendy   Cos it's like, not as if we don't know owt is it? We've
        gone through it all and that . . .
Wayne   There's all sorts now, you have these centres and
        things like that . . .
Wendy   Aye, and jobs . . . [a hint of resignation in her
        voice] . . . huh . . .
Wayne   We'd be happy to help wi' anything like that.
Wendy   It'd be alreet to start us own group up, wouldn't it,
        you know in this area. Cos there's nowt like that, is
        there at all?
Mother Well I don't think they only need it for't junkies,
        though, they need it for't parents an' all.
Wendy   Well that's all in, isn't it . . . it's all one thing . . .
Wayne   It would . . . round 'ere, it would . . .
Mother Definitely need it for't parents, cos I'll tell you
        sommat . . . I feel sorry for't junkies, but I feel sorry
        for . . . more sorrier for't parents . . . And some
        really, really try and help 'em, don't they? You
        know what I mean . . . and they get caught cold . . .
Wendy   Look outside, Cheryl . . . look at rain!

II
Decisions

I were always scared o't needle. And then I knocked about wi' this lass who were fixing. And one morning I didn't have any, and she did but it were in't works. So she said, 'Well, have half o' this . . . (Cheryl, 20 years, South Yorkshire)

I tried to sell it once. It was dead funny though like, I just took it . . . [laughs] . . . instead of selling it! . . . I just chased it all. (John, 19 years, Merseyside)

Like, say rob a jumper and then give it to someone, and they'll say, 'I'll give you four bags of smack' . . . Oh yeh, you can do that! That's what everyone does I think. (Sharon, 21 years, Merseyside)

I started robbin', robbed off my ma . . . I've done shoplifting and that like. But I've never robbed houses . . . I knew my limit . . . I couldn't rob a house, you know what I mean. Cos, like they're just the same class . . . (Eddie, 21 years, Merseyside)

I started going out on the game . . . No, I couldn't go shoplifting . . . I'd be too frightened of getting caught . . . On the street, I know what I'm doing. I do what I want to and nothing else, sort of thing. (Julie, 29 years, West Yorkshire)

101

Sticking a Needle in your Arm:
the Decision to Inject

Most people who use heroin in Britain today smoke it. As the new heroin problem began to gather momentum from the early 1980s onwards, this was a novel and significant departure within the British heroin culture where injection had previously been the dominant means of using the drug. The habit of smoking heroin, which had been previously quite unknown in Britain, had nevertheless been the preferred and traditional method of use in many other parts of the world. The practice of heating heroin powder on aluminium foil and inhaling the smoke through a tube had long been known in the Cantonese dialect of Hong Kong, for example, as *Júi Lùng*, or 'Chasing the Dragon'; placing the empty casing of a match box in the mouth in order to inhale the heroin fumes, on the other hand, is known somewhat jokingly as *Chúi Hou Kàm*, or 'Playing the Mouth Organ'.

It was, however, the expression 'chasing the dragon' which somehow caught on in Britain, and it was undoubtedly the recognition that imported 'brown' heroin could be smoked, when it first started to become available in cheap and plentiful supply between 1979 and 1981, which allowed the habit to spread with such rapidity in otherwise quite conventional neighbourhoods. A powerful cultural taboo against self-injection had been removed, and with it an increased likelihood that someone might be prepared to experiment with heroin.

Even so, intravenous self-injection (known as 'fixing', 'hitting it up', 'cranking up', 'jacking up', 'shooting', 'having a dig') is far from being extinct in Britain, and there are parts of the country where it either remains the dominant form of heroin use or co-exists with the newer practice of 'chasing', 'tooting' or 'dragoning'. Imported 'brown' heroin from Iran and the North-West Frontier is in fact a form of the drug prepared specifically for the purpose of smoking, and if it is to be rendered soluble for injection purposes then it must first be acidified. This is often done by means of a 'Jiff lemon', although a down-market version of the same procedure involves the use of vinegar. Just how it came to realized that heroin could be smoked and did not need to be injected is far from clear, but it signalled an important break with the earlier traditions of the 'junkie' subculture where injection itself had been both an important ceremonial aspect of a heroin user's initiation, as well as a major cultural barrier which had worked against the widespread dispersal of the heroin habit.

Smoking heroin is nevertheless without question an inefficient means of using the drug – quantities of it, quite literally, 'go up in smoke' – and as a user's dependence on and tolerance to heroin increases, there will be sometimes a temptation to switch to injection in order to reduce the financial costs of the habit. The experience of some heroin users suggests that if they begin to inject, then they can get by with a quarter of the amount of heroin which they had previously used when smoking. It is also often said that the initial 'rush' which the user experiences when injecting is more intense and pleasurable, offering a further incentive to switch to injecting.

Even so, there are obviously also costs to injecting as opposed to smoking heroin, in terms of various risks to health. When users share needles and syringes there is the risk of cross-infection by the AIDS virus. Heroin users who inject in this way will also risk hepatitis infection. Repeated self-injection causes untold damage to a person's veins, producing the tell-tale 'track marks' on a heroin user's arms. When opiates or other drugs are injected which are not intended for injection purposes (such as the opiate preparation Diconal, known as 'dikes', 'dikeys' or 'pinkies') then other forms of bodily damage can occur, such as abscesses, sores and boils, though these can also result from using needles that are unclean. Finally, heroin users who inject are undoubtedly much more likely to suffer overdoses than those who smoke the drug, sometimes resulting in death.

Whether heroin is smoked or injected, however, it is potentially addictive – contrary to the mistaken belief some-times held that heroin is less addictive when 'chased'. Nevertheless, in terms of a variety of other potential hazards, injection would seem to be a more dangerous practice than smoking, and a heroin user's decision whether or not to inject is by no means an unimportant one. But what is involved in this decision? So many times in the recollections of heroin users, we have seemed to be listening to people who were unaware that they were taking decisions about their lives as they slipped into their heroin habits. By a variety of subterfuges – 'you can't control it', 'it all happened so quickly', 'I didn't know', 'I didn't care' – people deny both their motives and their actions which led to addiction.

Sticking a needle in your arm, however, is an unmistakable decision, whichever way you care to look at it. And there are other decisions to be explored later: whether to get into the business of selling heroin; whether to turn to crime or prostitution to support your habit; and finally whether to 'come off' and then try to 'stay off' heroin. But first, the question of the needle.

Fears of needles: 'I just can't stand the sight of needles'

'I've never actually had a needle in my arm.'
  'Why's that?'
  'Well, like, ever since I've been a kid . . . like even if I go to the hospital now, and when they give me needles, I was like that . . . [grimaces] . . . I just can't stand needles . . . I suppose in the end, if I'd have carried on and that, I might've had a go. But like, I've even been there when people have done it like, and it just hasn't interested me. I just smoke it.' (Eddie, 21 years, Merseyside)

This is a typical response of one of the new heroin users who has never crossed the injection barrier. It rests its case on childhood fears of doctors and hospitals, or going to the dentist. For many people this is probably about as far as their curiosity about injection will take them.

> 'Needles? No . . . no fear of that with me, like. I just can't stand the sight of needles. I don't know what it is. Even when I were a kid, you know I used to have hay-fever and the doctor gave me this treatment . . . I'd tried the tablets and they didn't work, and it was injections, you know a course of injections . . . Oh no, I remember I cried all the way home, you know, I wouldn't go near the doctor again. I'd rather sneeze, like! You wouldn't get me even near a needle . . . But there's those that do. Like that lad round the corner from here, he's the only one that injects round here like, everyone else just has a toot. And you go round to his house . . . spoon always sticking out of the gas fire, the works on the kitchen table . . . Oh, he's a right mess . . . just too far gone.' (Colin, 23 years, Manchester)

The fear of needles must obviously be overcome if someone is to inject heroin, although even then there might be some residual anxieties. Here, for example, is a man who is not at all one of the new heroin users, but rather an old hand at the game who had injected heroin for maybe ten years:

> 'It's funny because, you know, I hate people sticking needles in me. I even fainted one time when I were in hospital for hepatitis, when I were given an injection by one o't nurses. Yet I could stick needles in myself all day, you know what I mean . . . in fact I have done!' (Gerry, 32 years, Manchester)

However, the decision whether or not to inject is not merely a question of overcoming the fear of needles. Nor is it only an individual matter, in that it will also be shaped by the styles of drug use already known within the locality where someone lives. An important consideration is whether injection techniques had been known and practised within the local drug culture prior to the arrival of heroin in the early 1980s: for example, whether or not barbiturates or amphetamine sulphate had been injected during the phase of 'poly-drug' use during the 1970s. In an area where amphetamine ('speed' or 'whizz') had been used in powder form and inhaled or 'snorted', when heroin first appeared the available repertoire of technologies for using powder drugs would not include injection, and it would be more likely to be smoked. Whereas, if the preferences of the local drug culture was to inject amphetamine, thus establishing a different technology for dealing with powders, then when heroin appeared on the scene it would not be uncommon for it to be injected from the first instance of use. For example:

Linda	You see up till then we'd been having, started having a bit of sulphate before then, didn't we?
Brian	Yeh.
Linda	And then a friend came round, said I couldn't get nowt, sulphate, so . . . got this heroin, and that was it.
Brian	That was it, that was't start.
Question	Did you smoke it then, or . . .
Brian	No I injected it.
Question	Straight away?
Brian	Straight away, cos I were injecting speed like first.
Question	Oh right.

(Linda and Brian, mid-20s, South Yorkshire)

Crossing the injection barrier is here described in casual, matter of fact terms, as an issue of little consequence. By contrast, from another locality where different patterns of drug experience had prevailed, we find a quite different attitude:

'I can't explain it like, you know, like cranking is the extent . . . you know what I mean. Like once you do that you're fucking, you're bad . . . y'know what I mean . . . you're sort of like, it's evil, you know what I mean, most people sort of regard it like that. Once you inject they think, "Oh fucking hell!" That's the furthest you can ever go like. And people are, y'know, frightened of doing that, and like they've still got a bit of self-respect not to do that.' (Keith, 20 years, Merseyside)

It is not that these different attitudes reflect the seriousness of the heroin problem in the two localities, as might be imagined from the offhand way in which Brian describes injection, as opposed to Keith's horrified response. On the contrary, Keith lives in an area where the heroin problem is undoubtedly much more serious and widespread than where Linda and Brian live. The differences originate in the established patterns of drug use within their local drug cultures, and also to some extent the availability of drugs. So that in the area of South Yorkshire where Linda and Brian come from, not only have injection techniques been an established part of the poly-drug culture for some time, but also a substantial proportion of the opiate drugs locally available consist not of imported 'brown' heroin but illicit pharmaceutical products, including morphine, Diconal, Palfium, pharmaceutically pure heroin and injectable methadone. Indeed, on Brian's reckoning, since the advent of imported 'brown' heroin in the locality significant numbers of people who had previously injected had switched to 'chasing'. Whereas in the Liverpool area, not only is imported heroin the drug most commonly available, but the pattern of heroin use has so far shown no real evidence of drifting away from the dominant pattern of smoking:

> 'I do know people who do inject it, but like the majority round here all smoke it. You get your few who, like . . . they don't mingle with the smackheads sort of thing . . . who do inject. They're registered drug addicts, they go to the clinic and get their amps, but they keep themselves to themselves. But all the rest, the one's that smoke it, that is the majority – I'd say like 95 per cent smoke it, not many inject.' (Paul, 24 years, Merseyside)

Taking the decision: 'It was mixed up ready to fix'

Nevertheless, although the local drug culture has an important influence in shaping people's decisions whether or not to inject, even within an area where smoking is the dominant form of use you will find individuals who do experiment with injection. Sometimes, people will switch almost entirely to injection as a preferred mode of heroin use. Others will try injecting from time to time, maybe out of curiosity, or they might resort to injecting heroin during times of a local shortage:

'I think the older ones like who've been on it a good few years, they get onto injecting. But the ones, say, from the last five or six years onwards . . . like most of them smoke. I think even people who smoke, though, like have a hit now and again. Just like if they're short on gear, they'll have a hit. It's not worth smoking £5 worth of gear and being withdrawing all the time, so they'll just inject it to get a better buzz off it. Then, like, you get those people O-D-ing, because they're not used to it, through injecting . . . It's just a big vicious circle isn't it?'

'Have you ever injected yourself?'

'I smoked it most of the time. Cos like I'm petrified of needles. But when I was short on money, I used to go like . . . Here's a £5 deal, make that do me for most of the day, you know, hitting it. Cos I wasn't used to hitting it, so it lasted longer. But like with chasing it, I was doing about a gram a day.' (Sharon, 21 years, Merseyside)

It is an important recognition that when someone experiments with injecting heroin on a very occasional basis, and where injection techniques remain a largely unknown terrain within the local drug culture, the risk of overdose is significantly higher. And whereas the powerful effects of injecting might be initially welcomed as a better 'buzz' or 'hit', they can also come to be experienced as somewhat frightening:

'No I've never, ever injected. No. I've only ever, you know, chased it with the foil . . .'

'Are there many people injecting?'

'No, not really. Not in Liverpool. There's a couple . . . you know, there's a few that'll try it, but they never stay at it like.'

'Why not?'

'I think most of my mates . . . I think they're scared of it, sort of thing. They've tried it, and they've said Oh it's the boss," you know, "it's great, it's the best way you can take it" and all that like. But . . . I think like they're just scared to have it every day. There's been a couple of mates who I know that, y'know, they've been injecting it for like a couple of weeks, and then they just . . . get afraid of the effects of injecting it, and they'll just stop and smoke it again like.' (Jack, 22 years, Merseyside).

It is once again sometimes a question of what people will be prepared to get into with friends. For just as friendship can overcome someone's initial reluctance to try heroin in the first place, it can also override their inhibitions against escalating their drug involvement by crossing the injection threshold, even when these inhibitions are quite strong. In any case, when heroin users start to inject, they will invariably need someone else to do it for them at first, either because they are afraid to inject themselves, or because they simply do not know what to do.

'There was only two of us, the only ones who injected it . . . I didn't like the idea, you know, not at all. I loved smoking it, but . . . Anyway, there was this mate who'd tried it and said he knew this lad who could do it, and it was great, sort of thing. But it's a little bit . . . you know . . . and both of us just knocked it on the head. It's too heavy. But we tried it.'
'Did you get syringes easily enough?'
'Yeh. Easy. I used to go into the chemist and say I'm a diabetic, I need the needles . . .
'Did you share needles?'
'We used the same works, but changed the needle. Because my mate had one of those, what do you call them . . . Mm . . . I don't know what it was, but it was dead easy to change the needle. And we just done that, for ages.'
'And you never got hepatitis or anything like that?'
'No, He was dead clean, the person who used to do me was really clean, like. He'd throw out the spoon every day, and change everything. He was dead clean that lad. And then we started doing it ourselves. But like it was . . . one morning, what made me really stop it, injecting . . . I woke

up and done it. I woke up, set it out and just done it. First
thing in the morning, to do it like that! Stoned and all. I
couldn't believe that. Because I didn't need it. It was just
like . . . what I used to do was inject about £15's worth a day
and I'd chase another twenty. Like cos I still loved chasing it.
But putting a needle in your arm, I didn't like it. I didn't like
it one bit.' (Joey, 20 years, Merseyside)

If friendship can be one form of inducement towards
experimenting with injection techniques, then the availability
of heroin can be another, where it is perhaps only immediately
available to an addict in an injectable form. Cheryl, who
admitted to a 'greedy' heroin habit which eventually involved
both smoking and injecting heroin, remembered the first time
that she had ever injected:

Cheryl I were smoking it for ages, I never touched a fix in
      my life. I were always scared o't needle. And then I
      knocked about wi' this lass who were fixing. And
      one morning I didn't have any, and she did but it
      were in't works. So she said, 'Well have half o'
      this' . . .
Wayne That's what I think, that's how I think it happens
      most o't time missen, wi't company sort of thing,
      y'know one thing leads to a bigger thing, doesn't it?'
                 (Cheryl, 20 years, South Yorkshire)

A woman from another part of Yorkshire, who had also
developed a heavy heroin habit through 'chasing', described
her own initiation into injecting in identical terms:

'The first time I used a needle was . . . I was coming down
really badly and I had no heroin and I went round to a
friend's house who I thought would have some. And this
chap said that, yes, he did have some but he'd just mixed it
up in a spoon and put it in a syringe. And he said I could
have half of it, but it was mixed up ready to fix. So, you
know, he said that he would fix me with half of this if I
wanted it, and it was either that or nothing. So that was the
first . . .'
  'He injected you?'

'Yeh.'

'What was it like?'

'Oh . . . [laughs] . . . it was really nice.'

'Was it better than smoking?'

'Yeh . . . Because you've got this very strong initial rush off it . . . just a really nice sensation. But that was just a one-off. I didn't start using the needle regularly until months later . . . January of this year.' (Julie, 29 years, West Yorkshire)

The similarity of these two stories provokes the thought that maybe we are listening to another of those moral subterfuges by which heroin users deny their own actions and motives, saying in effect, 'it wasn't me that did it, it was the drug.' Nevertheless, as Julie herself said, she did not begin to inject regularly for some time after this, and when she did it was the result of a consciously motivated decision to reduce the cost of her habit. Julie was someone who had quickly developed a voracious appetite for heroin after being introduced to it by friends, so that she and her boyfriend were smoking one and a half grams of heroin daily within a matter of months – and hers was the lion's share. In order to support her habit, which was costing her something in the region of £600 to £700 per week, she had turned to prostitution. At first, being a prostitute did not seem to worry her at all – it was easy money. But then, for a variety of reasons, she lost enthusiasm for the trade and became desperately short of money. This was when she started to inject:

'Well basically . . . I went off going out on the street for some reason and I didn't have much money, and I found that I could really only afford about a £10 bag a day. And chasing that wasn't doing me any good whatsoever. I was still feeling . . . you know, it wasn't enough even to hold me, you know, just take away the symptoms of coming down. It just wasn't enough when I was chasing, so I started injecting it. At first I had to get other people to do it for me, I couldn't do it, but then I started trying to do it myself . . .'

'How long was it before you started injecting yourself?'

'Not very long, a few weeks. Because I found that I liked

it, and if there was no one there to do it for me, then I just . . . I got someone to show me how to do it, but I mean I'm not very good at it. You can see the mess of this arm, and that's after . . . what . . . six months, seven months . . . [laughs] . . . I can still make a mess of myself! I know people who've been injecting for years and they haven't got a mark on them, but . . .'

'So did that stabilize you, then, when you started injecting?'

'I find now that I'll take as much, more or less, up to a certain point . . . I'll take as much heroin as I can get my hands on, as I can afford. But then it makes me feel bad if I have too much. So I have a sort of limit to the amount I can take without, you know, it having the opposite effect of making me feel sick and headachey and bad . . . I think if I have more than a quarter of a gram a day, it's getting on for being too much. But over last summer . . . I was chasing sometimes a gram a day, and it wasn't having that effect on me, it wasn't making me ill.'

Julie was therefore able to reduce the cost of her heroin habit to a quarter of what it had been before she began to inject. This did not mean, however, that financial costs were the only consideration. She worried about the health risks associated with injecting, for example, and her boyfriend also disapproved of her using the needle:

'No, no, he doesn't, he doesn't approve at all. He's always . . . every time I get a needle out he gives me hell. I'm very strong willed, like, and I won't let him stop me. But I get a hard time for it, which I'm glad about really because it does make me think about it. And you know, I'd like to stop injecting because it's . . . I mean there's so many dangers, there's hepatitis to think about, there's . . . all sorts of things.'

When heroin users begin to inject, they face a number of vital decisions in terms of what health precautions they should take. However, given that people are so often left to their own devices in these matters – because although our society understands the need to offer education and instruction in proper injection techniques to diabetics, for example, the idea that we should do the same for heroin addicts is somehow beyond the pale – their health precautions are often built on very shaky foundations.

Brian	Oh yeh, there were no trouble getting works. Cos like, wi' people swiping 'em from't hospital, and you know we were getting 'em from all ovver. People had cards to go and buy 'em from't chemist and that . . . it were no trouble at all. But like . . . we didn't use brand new needles, we used same one again and again and again and again . . . But luckily we never got owt bad, we never got hepatitis, or . . .'
Linda	No, no.
Brian	We never got any disease from it or owt, you know, because we were still clean weren't we?
Linda	Yeh.
Brian	Even though we used . . .
Question	Did you have one each?
Brian	We used't same. You know, we didn't let anybody else use it like. It were just ours, mine and Linda's like.
Linda	Yeh.
Brian	So that's probably why we didn't get any disease . . . I mean, like, I've seen . . . there's these two brothers, well they're not, they're step-brothers . . . and they wouldn't even bother cleaning't blood out. They used to just, have same . . . Like stick it in one . . .
Linda	Cos they were brothers, they thought it were alright.
Brian	. . . Pull't blood in, whap half of it in their arm, take it out and then go onto next un . . . I just couldn't believe it me. I wouldn't even dare do it wi' Linda, you know I wouldn't even dare to put Linda's blood in me . . . I mean even though it'd be alright like.

(Linda and Brian, mid-20s, South Yorkshire)

From Liverpool, Sharon reported that rumours about the possibility of AIDS infection had introduced an element of caution into the injecting scene, so that sharing needles became rare:

> 'Everyone's got their own needle now. Cos like they used to just pass the needle round and that, and they was ending up with hepatitis and all of that. And now with the addicts ending up with AIDS and that like, it's just quieting back a bit now like and they're just using their own needles . . .'
>
> 'Is it easy to get needles?'
>
> 'Oh you can get them easy enough. You've only got to go down to the chemists and ask for diabetic needles, or whatever it is . . . syringes . . . And like as I say, there's people selling 'em, the glass ones or the plastic ones. The plastic ones go for £2.50 and the glass ones for a fiver . . . But like if they're turkeying, who's gonna give you a fiver? It's murder . . .' (Sharon, 21 years, Merseyside)

This, one fears, is an account of someone not too well acquainted with the injection scene. Sharon's view that a heroin user would always prefer to spend £5 on heroin, rather than on a clean syringe, is no doubt sound, but her reassurances that people were now taking care never to share needles has something of a hollow ring. Because, whatever good intentions people might start out with when they enter into injecting heroin, it so often seems that caution is eventually thrown to the wind. Julie, for example, remembered her own experience clearly enough:

> 'When I first started to think about fixing, I used to think that I would have my own glass syringe, and I would sterilize it every time and I would never use anyone else's works and I would never let anyone else . . . you know . . . and that lasted about a week. And then, you just fall into the habits of everyone else which is, eh, you know, sharing works, using the same works as other people . . .' (Julie, 29 years, West Yorkshire)

Cheryl and Wendy from South Yorkshire described how they cherished similar ambitions which had suffered the same fate, although their account was flavoured with their own sense of grim comedy:

Question Did you share needles or did you have your own?

Cheryl Well, one bit, we bought this diabetic card. And we used to go and get 'em every week. Clean works, every new fix . . . [sighs] . . . It used to be lovely. But I've used some awful works, me, you know where it's all broke off and . . . got spaghetti to get plunger out, and . . .

Mother Aye, spaghetti all o'er my stairs!

Cheryl . . . Butter, putting butter in it so it'll come out easy . . .

Wendy Aye, margarine inside't works, it used to look horrible didn't it?

Cheryl Ooh, you wonder why you didn't get owt off it, hepatitis and that like . . .

Wendy When I used to fix, I used to go like that me . . . [grimaces] . . . I couldn't look.

(Cheryl and Wendy, early 20s, South Yorkshire)

Dealing, Hustling and Robbing

Usually, we think only of heroin as an addiction. But it is also a currency in a vast economic system. This is an economy which stretches around the world, linking such otherwise dissimilar places and lifestyles as those of the street users of the ghettos in New York and the drab streets of Liverpool, with poor peasant farmers in the opium poppy fields of the North-West Frontier or Thailand, via the laboratories and trade routes of India, Pakistan and formerly the notorious 'French connection' of Marseilles (cf. Henman, et al., 1985). This global heroin economy is not only immense (although not nearly so immense as that of cannabis which is a major cash-crop now for many Third World countries and also some states of the USA) but also highly lucrative for those who can situate themselves at the right point within it. At other points within this complex system of distribution and exchange, however, among the worker-ants of the heroin economy, very little money is made at all; but nevertheless, even at 'street level' heroin is surrounded by a constant flurry of economic exchanges, whether in the form of small-scale drug-dealing, robbing and thieving, prostitution, or a myriad of other forms of daily hustle.

From rags to rags:
'Just to support their habit sort of thing'

At the point of production, in the poppy fields, the money to be made by peasant farmers can vary dramatically from year to

117

year, according to the quantity and quality of the harvest. Nevertheless, the farmers will always receive only a tiny fraction of what the opium crop will realize when it is turned into heroin. So, too, at the level of the small 'user-dealer' there is little money to be made. The commanding heights of the heroin economy lie in between these two extremes of subsistence economics, in the shadowy world of international trafficking, smuggling and multi-kilogram heroin transactions. The profits in this sphere of economic activity can be immense. In the early 1980s, for example, one kilogram of heroin could be bought at the North-West Frontier for between £3,000 and £4,000 – although the peasant farmers might have received no more than a couple of hundred pounds for the ten kilograms of opium which it would have taken to produce that kilo of heroin.

This same kilogram of heroin might then be transported to Europe at an overall cost of maybe £7,000, including all overheads for transportation and couriers. On arrival in Britain, its value will have trebled, to something in excess of £20,000 – a quiet profit of £13,000 on a £7,000 outlay. Or, if that kilogram of heroin were then traded down in ounces (with 35 ounces to the kilo, and a going rate something in the region of £1,000 per ounce) its value would have increased to maybe £35,000 or more. These are all rough sums, but they are the kinds of profits that a prospective heroin importer will be looking at.

Then, that same ounce which might have been purchased for £1,200 (prices always fluctuate in this risky market place) becomes 28 grams to be sold at £70 per gram, at a profit on this basis of £800 without even allowing for the fact that the heroin will now have been diluted or 'cut' with talcum-powder or glucose somewhere along the way. In fact, the metric conversion tables no longer have any meaning in these lower reaches of the heroin economy. The 35 ounce kilogram has become maybe 40 ounces of diluted heroin. The 28 gram ounce becomes 35 grams. And so on, down to the milligram quantities which appear in the £5 'bag' or 'wrap' which is knocked out from a user-dealer's flat in a run-down area of town. And here other adulterants begin to make their appearance: pepper, brick-dust and even flux to make the heroin 'run' more easily on the smoker's foil so that it appears to be unadulterated. But by now, heroin has become a subsistence economy once again. The major cash gains, in the upper reaches of the economy, are made only through kilo and multi-kilo deals, and less spectacularly but nevertheless substantially by those who deal in quantities of an ounce or thereabouts.

At the highest level the market attracts both established criminal organizations and 'mafias', where people have sufficient capital to set up in the global trafficking business, as well as smaller-scale entrepreneurial ventures of a more fitful nature. Someone who could successfully arrange to import a kilogram of heroin which is then sold in Britain, could stand to make something in the region of £14,000 clear profit on a £7,000 outlay, even if this were still traded on in bulk as a kilogram. If they were prepared to deal this down in ounces, then even without cutting, a £7,000 outlay would yield a return of £35,000 or maybe £40,000. Someone prepared to take that risk three times would have made a cool profit of £100,000. Even when an imported kilo is only passed on as a kilo, five transactions would yield a profit of £70,000. These are large pickings, through which a handful of kilogram transactions could generate sufficient capital to set someone up in a legitimate business in a small, but lucrative way. Then, when sufficient capital has been accumulated, heroin trafficking ceases to be a matter of concern, having served its purpose – or at least, that is the theory of short-term, entrepreneurial dabbling in the heroin economy.

We know very little, however, about how these major kilo and multi-kilo heroin transactions are carried out, or who they are carried out by. The people who stand to make such substantial profits will often only put up the money, and maybe never even see the heroin itself. Moreover, it is probably unusual for people who operate in the commanding heights to use heroin themselves. It is only down at the messy end of the heroin business that we begin to glimpse what is going on:

'Most of the ones, all round here like, there's a few big time dealers, but the rest of them are just out for their own smoke. Cos like, you know some of these big ones that you hear about, like who bring it into the country . . . and them that sell a quarter ounce and what have you . . . they don't normally take it themselves; it's just, like, the little ones, that sell it and get it for their own smoke and that. But you've gotta watch what you're getting though, cos everyone's cutting it back, like with brick-dust . . . Like you buy a fiver, and you get a bag full of brick-dust, you know, pepper and everything, sherbert . . . If you're getting like half ounces, if you can afford that like, you know you're gonna get the right gear. Maybe it's been cut a little bit, a bit of talc or something . . . but when you get some of these round here . . . sherbert, brick-dust . . . I wonder why everyone's not O-D-ing themselves and that like, putting all that shite into their arm . . . I've had some stuff, too, that smelt really weird . . . I don't know what it was, but it gave you a terrible head in the morning.' (Sharon, 21 years, Merseyside)

You hear the same stories wherever you go in the lower reaches of the heroin economy:

Cheryl They're cutting it wi' all sorts round here, shit we've had honest . . . I've had it wi', er, what tasted like mothballs.

Wendy They'll cut it wi' out . . . glucose . . . reet sweet.

Cheryl And there were hennah in it, like straw when you put it in't spoon.

(Cheryl and Wendy, early 20s, South Yorkshire)

'Anyone who hits up that kind of gear is looking for an early grave. No, when the "brown" heroin came in, I packed in the needle. I mean a sore arm's one thing, but who needs a place in Moston cemetry? My ma's got her name down for there, like, but I'm not ready for that. You know what I mean?' (Alan, 24 years, Manchester)

'See, when I first started getting into smack it was dead good, like now it's *last* . . . It's not proper smack. Ages ago, it was, cos there wasn't that many people on it. And like it was good then, it was good smack then like. But, er, if you went down there now and got a bag, you'd never know what was in it, they're selling all kinds of muck. Like, I'd be alright, because I know 'em all. But if they think they could put one over on you, like, they would. Deffo.' (John, 19 years, Merseyside)

'When it first came round and that like, the fivers you got were a lot bigger, cos like no-one was hardly touching it then . . . And if you got a weighed gram, at that time, it *was* a weighed gram, you know, there was nobody sticking tubes to the scales and all that . . . And yeh, even the gear was better, no-one was cutting it to make the money and that like. Just satisfied with what they were getting. But now, like, you get a £5 deal and you never know what you're getting.' (Gail, 20 years, Merseyside)

These petty little tricks are part of the desperate effort to eke out an existence in the lowest reaches of the heroin economy. Here is how one ex-user described how user-dealers that he had known would operate from day to day:

'They'll buy a gram, which'll cost 'em from £60 to £75. Now what they'll do is cut £70 worth, say, into £5 or £10 bags. The rest of what's left of the gram is their smoke for the day. They go sell that £70 of gear . . . well, that's enough for the next gram. And so on. You see, not making any money, but just supplying their habit sort of thing . . . and like, the more they can cut the gram, the more their own smoke is . . . Doing that, you know, from day to day like.' (Keith, 20 years, Merseyside)

This is undoubtedly one of the lowest levels of a heroin distribution network, describing the 'typical' activity of a user-dealer or user-supplier through which no surplus profits are made, and where the aim is simply to supply one's own habit. Viewed in one light it is simply a hand-to-mouth 'subsistence' economy. However, if we look at it from a cash-flow viewpoint, then this economic activity takes on a rather different complexion. If this user-dealer were able to sustain his £70 per day transaction for a full year, it would represent an annual cash-flow of £25,000 and he would have knocked out something like one-third of a kilogram of heroin. It would still be true that he would not be making any cash profit out of his low-level business, and he would remain as poor as a church mouse. Nevertheless, it takes little imagination to see that in a deprived neighbourhood with high unemployment levels, an annual cash-flow of £25,000 is a phenomenal achievement. With something like £500 per week passing through his pockets, this young man would in all probability be a figure of some real local standing. There would always be a little spare cash around, perhaps. He would be the man to know if you wanted to score a 'bag', because even if he did not have any immediately available heroin himself, he would possess a good working knowledge of the local 'smack' scene. Indeed, whether we prefer to think of him as a resourceful entrepreneur, or as an abject victim of the heroin traffic, locally he would undoubtedly be 'Jack the Lad'. Or at least, that is the promise which is held out to someone who contemplates becoming involved in small-scale heroin deals.

The problem is that, quite apart from the long arm of the law, unless user-dealers are able to keep their own heroin habits in check – which is probably unlikely – their business enterprise will come crashing down around their ears. John from Liverpool remembered the fiasco when he decided to chance his hand at dealing:

'I tried to sell it once. It was dead funny though like, I just took it . . . [laughs] . . . instead of selling it! You know, me and this lad went halves and bought two grams, and then he got arrested. So I just chased it all [laughs] . . . He got out of the cells two days later, and he went mad. I was sitting there like that . . . you know really wrecked. "Where's all the money?" I said, "I've got a tenner here, you can lend it" and threw it at him . . . It's just like, you can go down there and sell it in ten minutes, or you can go down and wait for two hours and sell nothing. I talked to a lad down there about a week ago, he sold about £300 and he did it in no time . . . a quarter of an hour, and £150 of it's his, so he made £150 in fifteen minutes . . . But like I went down there, and in let's say half an hour I'd only sold £10 worth, so I just went home and took it all!' (John, 19 years, Merseyside)

A large amount of heroin dealing at this low level is done from the user-dealer's own house or flat, although in some towns and cities there are pubs where it is possible to score heroin and other illicit drugs. When conditions such as these prevail, it is obviously a fairly tight market which is not easy to break into. In order to sell from one's own house with any measure of success, for example, it will be necessary to have first established a local reputation, and this will take time. A buyer will also need an introduction:

Question I mean, could you just go up, knock on the door and buy some?
Cheryl   No, no . . .
Wendy   Somebody'd have to take you who they know.
Wayne   You go in't pubs and you meet people, and then you get into going back to somebody's house, you know what I mean. And then, there's everybody crashed out in't house. And you think like, your first impression, "What's going off like?" And then, there's blow going about like . . . And then if you keep going back to't same places, pubs and that like, you get to find out what things are for yourself, you know what I mean? That's how you get introduced to it.
(Cheryl, Wayne and Wendy, early 20s, South Yorkshire)

When John had decided to try his hand at selling some heroin, on the other hand, he had been able to take himself off to a place where £5 and £10 bags were bought and sold in the open street. Another heroin user from the same locality described a typical scene in the vicinity of a block of flats where street-dealing was commonplace:

'You go in the area, like, and there's about . . . at the most about six people selling it there, you know, it's like a market. You walk in, "You're after gear?" "Don't buy his gear, buy mine!" "Here you are, mine's the best bags, here y'are look at these!" "Fuck off, I've seen 'im first!" And all that, like.

That's what it's like as you walk by. Like a big market stall.
(Jack, 22, Merseyside)

This was an area which had become so notorious that people
were travelling from wide distances in order to both buy and
sell heroin:

'Normally, if you can't get gear round here there's none
anywhere . . . I mean, people are coming from all over now.
It's got that way, there's loads of 'em selling, you feel as if it
were a fishmarket. "Here y'are girl, do you want gear?" . . .
Like I've seen queues down there, when there's a bit of a
drought on. Honest to god . . . [laughs] . . . it's mad. You
know if you go over there, turkeying, it's one o'clock . . . the
gear isn't gonna be there until five. You go back over
there . . . there's crowds of people in front of you up the
stairs, fighting for the gear like . . . lads at the back with the
bags and what have you. It's mad.'
'So could anyone just go down and buy it?'
'Well, some of them won't sell to people they don't know.
But down there, the DS [drug squad] are known like, you
see them running after someone every day. You've gotta
laugh at them like, because it's the same ones all the time. So
like, as soon as they come on the estate like, "Here, it's the
DS, get off!" . . . So like, they're just well known.'
'So anyone could buy it?'
'Probably, it all depends . . . I mean like, if you went over
there and said like, "Have you got a bag?", you'd probably
get one . . . get it easy like . . . Course . . . [laughs] . . .
you'd also get mugged if there's someone turkeying behind
you like!' (Sharon, 21 years, Merseyside)

What is being described here is a form of street-trading not at
all unlike what is known in North America as a 'copping area',
although it is probably unusual for heroin to be sold quite so
openly in Britain. What one does find in some towns and
cities, however, are areas where it is well known that cannabis
is bought and sold openly in the street – often in the vicinity of
black communities. Sometimes heroin users had imagined that
they could go along to these areas to buy heroin, and were

surprised to find their requests greeted with a blunt refusal, together with a certain amount of disapproval and even hostility:

Question Do you get many blacks involved?

Wendy No, it's just blow with them, isn't it? That's all they're into . . .

Cheryl Well, we went to Bradford one time . . . I were telling you there were this drought on . . . and we went to this pub, cos we'd heard that it were theer. We'd read in't papers that you could get smack there, you know. And we stood outside like, and all these black kids were running up to us, 'Sensimilia!', 'Black!', and all this palavah . . . you know, they had all sorts o' blow, all sorts . . . Anyway, we were saying, 'No, we want smack' . . . Oh, they were off their heads . . . No way.

(Cheryl and Wendy, early 20s, South Yorkshire)

Paul had a similar experience when he went to visit a distant city:

'I went to Leeds to stay with my cousin, like. And while I was up there I went to this place the next day . . . you know, I wanted gear. And I went to this place, it was like a ghetto and there was this big community building with all the negroes hanging about, all the coloureds hanging out. And I went there, and they openly sold, you know, draw and what have you. But when I asked for smack, they were almost like shocked, you know what I mean, like "Oh you'll not get none o' that round here". And one of them give me a lecture, you know for about an hour, on smack and different types of drugs. But they just didn't want to know about smack . . . But like I say, they were openly selling everything else . . .' (Paul, 24 years, Merseyside)

Paul should have known better, perhaps, because even in his own city it was well known among heroin users that in the black community of Liverpool 8, or Toxteth, heroin was unavailable. Indeed, at the time when another Merseyside neighbourhood, Croxteth, was gaining some notoriety in the local press on account of its heroin problem, there were vivid graffiti in Liverpool 8, declaring 'This is Toxteth, Not Croxteth. No Smack!' Sometimes, in fact, when people tried to buy heroin in black communities where cannabis was freely available they got more than they bargained for, and it was not just a lecture:

'I've been all over the place to score.'
 'What about Toxteth?'
 'Oh no, you don't go down there like. There's no gear down there . . . no way. I know some who've tried. But . . . it's just the darkies trying to rip you off and that. I know a lad who went down there, he was at the clinic like. He went down, trying to score . . . must have been desperate or something . . . and the darkies done him in. Robbed his money like. "Oh you want smack?", like. "Here y'are, come in here", you know. Then . . . bang! Like I say, just done him in, give him hell of a beating, robbed his money . . . Like, "Don't come round here no more, asking for smack." No, they're not into it, you know. Only mugs go down there, like, what don't know nothing.' (Eddie, 21 years, Merseyside)

It was generally agreed, in fact, that although cannabis dealers operated with a certain degree of freedom within some black communities, they showed little or no interest in heroin. For some people who lived in neighbourhoods where heroin had become a common currency, this could even be source of puzzlement:

'I knew some black lads from school and that. And then you get the Rastas, like, you know who're always blasted out of their heads on draw and what have you. But smack? No, they don't want to know . . . It's like, I don't know, it's . . . it's weird really. Like, they're just happy with their ghetto blasters and their draw aren't they? And their roller skates and that . . . [laughs] . . .' (Jack, 22 years, Merseyside)

If there were sharp divisions in these people's experiences between cannabis and heroin dealing networks, then within

the heroin economy itself there were other important distinc-
tions to be made. For example, between those who deal in
heroin in order to support their own habits as against those
who do not use heroin themselves. Jack, who experienced
some difficulty in understanding why black people who were
involved in cannabis dealing should shun heroin, could
describe this other distinction clearly enough:

> 'The ones who are just making the money, they call them the
> "breadheads", like . . . Smackheads are the ones who're
> after the smack, like, and breadheads are the ones who are
> after the money . . .'

Although heroin users will often express the view that it is
wrong for people who do not use heroin themselves to supply
it, they know that ultimately their own supply depends on
such people, and that there are necessarily points at which
'breadheads' and 'smackheads' must meet. In some of the
more open street-dealing operations, in fact, one can begin to
glimpse something of the complexity of the heroin economy
and the division of labour that is involved, connecting sources
of substantial supply with the trade in £5 bags or wraps. For
example:

> 'You've got people coming over who've just got the grams,
> you know, and who are just doing it for their own habit.
> And they come over every day with their gram. They cut the
> gram, like, they'll sell that, they go back to wherever they're
> bagging the gram up and do that so many times a day to
> support their habit. And then you've got your other type,
> your plain breadheads, who come down and . . . you know
> the smackheads who just like hang around the area and all
> that, they'll give them, "Here you are, here's £200 worth of
> gear," like, "take thirty quid's worth yourself, sell that I'll be
> back in two hours" . . . Pick the money up, he'll give you
> more. That sort of thing.' (Paul, 24 years, Merseyside)

In Paul's view this was an entirely common form of
transaction in the area in which he lived, although it was also
one from which he derived a distinction in his own mind
between the victims of the system and the real villains:

'It's alright the police coming down and picking, y'know, the punters up, and catching them with £5 bags and nicking them and all that. But they're not getting the right people are they? . . . Some of them, you know, have got it really boxed off where they don't even actually touch the gear. You know, they front the money to buy the ounce or whatever, a few ounces. Someone'll pick it up, someone'll cut it up, someone'll take it down, someone'll sell it . . . and that person might not actually see or touch the gear, you know what I mean. And the higher you get up in the ladder sort of thing . . . they just finance it, and reap the benefits sort of thing. And then, like, the people who are dependent on gear, who because like they haven't got any money and they're always skint, they'll sell £200 worth in a couple of hours, you know to get £30 worth of smoke themselves, and they'll do that four or five times a day, making someone £1,000 a day, no bother. There's some money there.'

Sometimes users took the view that those who deal in the drug without using it themselves derived a kind of perverse pleasure in the business of watching the user grovel:

Wendy   There isn't many people that are dealing heroin what don't use it thissens.

Question I was going to ask you that, are they nearly all users?

Wendy   I know one person.

Cheryl   Yeh, I know one too.

Wayne   But he's locked up now . . .

Wendy   Aye, but he were dealing it for ages, weren't he Cheryl? But he never used it.

Cheryl   Like at Christmas, there weren't none at all, everyone were turkeying . . .

Wendy   And he were feeding his bird, weren't he Cheryl, weren't he?

Cheryl   He loved it, him, you know, he loved to see you turkeying . . . begging . . . you know when it really gets to you.

Wendy   Weren't he, feeding his bird, like.. He had a bird and she were an addict . . . and he used to gee her loads, didn't he?

Cheryl I couldn't sell it . . . like, you know, if I weren't a
user, I wouldn't dream of selling it me, God, it's
evil that . . . It used to get me right mad, cos like
at Christmas, such as Christmas, you'd be looking
for it . . . every day I went looking for it, I
wouldn't gee up . . .

Wendy There weren't much about, were there?

Cheryl There weren't none about, all over . . . well, we
got bits now and again. And we used to go up to
him, like, cos he were't main dealer then, and
we'd say 'When are you getting something?' And
he'd be laughing, like, in your face, seeing you
turkeying.

Wendy But like, he's never earnt nowt out of it really; he's
never got nowt out of it, so I can't see . . . you
know everybody were always ripping him off.

Cheryl I remember once, right, somebody sneaked in't
house while he were in bed! And got his trousers,
on't side of't bed . . . 4 gram o' smack, I think, and
about 300-and-odd quid . . . from't side of his bed
while he were laid in there, like . . .

(Cheryl, Wayne and Wendy, early 20s, South Yorkshire)

Stories such as these which circulate within the heroin scene
remind you sometimes of the Wild West. And whether they
are true or not, or what elements of truth are woven with
rumour and gossip, is always a matter for speculation – and
maybe even beside the point. In this case the story served a
wonderful purpose, whether true or false, as a moment of
conversational revenge against a 'wicked' non-using dealer.
From another part of Yorkshire, we hear a similar character
assassination of dealers, although this time without the
element of revenge. Nor was it only dealers who did not use
heroin themselves who were disliked, but all of them:

'I don't know any people round here who don't use it as
well . . . I've known a few people who've started out not
using it and selling it, but eventually they've started taking it
and ended up with habits themselves . . . But I've never got
into dealing it. And I wouldn't deal it. I'll be responsible for
one habit, but . . . and I've seen how people go who are

dealers, they turn into very nasty horrible people.'

'Do they? Why's that?'

'I don't know what it is . . . whether they're initially very nasty horrible people anyway, but they all seem to . . . I don't know . . . they're strange, strange, weird people. You can go along to them, coming down . . . really badly you know, and they'll make you sit and wait. You know, wind you up and things like that if you go to score off them. They get off on it, the ego thing of being "The Man", you know the dealer. And to start off they'll be selling freely from their houses, and then all of a sudden, well, "If you want it, you'll have to go to so-and-so because I'm not selling it from the house any more", and things like that . . .'

'What else do they get up to? Do they try and push the price up and get more money out of you?'

'Not really, it's a pretty standard thing the price, you know . . . It goes up and down a bit, but . . . Mind you, the price round here is absolutely ludicrous at the moment. About a year ago you could go and buy a weighed gram of heroin for £55. And now, I could go today and buy one and it would cost me £130. The bloke who was selling it before for £55 got bust, you see, and afterwards there was a bit of a shortage for a while. And then the people who did get their hands on it to sell wouldn't even sell . . . wouldn't sell weighed grams or a weighed quarter gram or half-grams or anything. All they would sell were £10 bags, £5 bags. Which meant, you know, they were drawing out about £200 or £300 on a gram which if they were going and buying a quarter ounce out of town was, say, £350, £50 a gram . . . you know making colossal amounts of money, £200 or £300 for a gram that only cost them £50. And they know that you'll take anything; I mean sometimes I've gone and paid £10; for a tiny, tiny little bit of heroin that I knew wasn't going to make me feel . . . Well, psychologically it was going to make me feel better. But it was nothing like the amount that I would need to take all the symptoms away.' (Julie, 29 years, West Yorkshire)

At the bottom end of the heroin market, there is an assumption that when users and user–dealers are doing business among themselves, even though the heroin will be 'cut' with dilutants, there will be a residue of fairness in these transactions: 'they are only doing it to supply their own habits.' But where the different worlds of the 'smackheads' and the 'breadheads' intersect there can be awkward tensions within the heroin economy, because where making money is the operating principle then the rules change. Indeed, sometimes the rules can become awfully rough:

'As I say, when I first got into it I had money then, I had a few bob. A good job, like, and a few bob saved. So that when I actually started buying it, when I was really hooked on it, I was spending like £200 a day on it. You know, I spent a few thousand pounds in no time at all . . . Like, I had a car, sold that. Jewellery, and what money I had in the bank, and you know my girl's money as well . . . it was our money sort of thing for the house. Spent that. But because I was, er, like spending £100, £200 a day sort of thing, every day in and day out, I was going to the dealers and like . . . they knew that I had money and I was a good customer, so when my money did run out I was getting my gear laid on. You know, like up front. So like, I got into a lot of debt, like £800 debt . . . and there was trouble over that.'
'What kind of trouble?'
'They took me . . . took me in a car . . . to where there was this beach where all the sand dunes are, took me there, beat me up with sticks, cut my hair and all that . . .'
'What, the dealers?'
'Yeh. You see that's how a lot of people get trapped into actually selling gear, they get in that much debt the only way they can get out of it is the dealer saying, "Well here y'are, you owe us this much. You go out and sell this much and we'll knock so much off your bill" . . . I mean, like I was spending a lot. I must have spent £4,000 or £5,000 on it . . . But at the end when my money'd gone, you know what I mean, they'd trapped me sort of thing . . . Well, that's how I see it now. Like . . . the only way I could've got out of it is if I turned round and started selling it, you know what I mean. But there was no way I'd risk three or four years by selling it . . . Alright I've used it, but selling's a different thing. As I

say, I saw a lot of people get caught that way into selling it, and they're the ones who get nicked and are doing three or four years. But they're not the main ones, you know what I mean, they're only supplying their habit. They're not actually making money, it's the ones who are higher up, like the ones who beat me up and that. They don't actually use it.' (Paul, 24 years, Merseyside)

Thieving: 'I never robbed a house, like, I knew my limit'

Not everybody who gets involved with the heroin scene turns to dealing in order to support their habits, although as we have seen the heroin distribution network requires a small army of people who are prepared to handle the drug if it is to work successfully at the lowest level. Indeed, although heroin users will often invoke a morality which says that it is only the people who deal in large quantities of the drug without using it themselves, and not the user–dealers, who are really doing wrong, it is nevertheless possible to argue the other way that if it were not for the small user–dealers heroin would simply become unavailable in a neighbourhood, because the risks of street-dealing are simply unacceptable for people who count their drug transactions in tens of thousands of pounds. Without the small hustles of the worker-ants in this economy, it is entirely possible that the heroin trade would significantly contract.

Other ways of supporting a heroin habit, of course, include burglary, shoplifting and theft. Although again, not everyone who uses heroin will be prepared to take such risks:

Brian I couldn't do it me, I wouldn't have't guts . . . not even if I were turkeying really bad, I couldn't do that. Well, we didn't did we?

Linda No.

Brian I just couldn't . . .

(Linda and Brian, mid-20s, South Yorkshire)

And as well as those who simply never get involved in crime, there are also people such as Wendy who found that shoplifting was such a torment that she stopped taking heroin:

'I used to shoplift, but I were scared o' doing't shoplifting, scared o' getting caught . . . And that stopped me from using . . . I wouldn't risk my liberty like.' (Wendy, 21 years, South Yorkshire)

Other people sit uneasily on the margins of crime, sometimes finding it hard to recollect how they did actually manage to support their habits:

'I think the most I've ever been on, generally it would have been about half a gram at the most. I'd say about £20 a day, like. But there's been a few times when I've had like half a gram a day and that.'

'So how did you manage to pay for it, were you thieving?'

'Phhh . . . I don't really know to be honest. That's always like . . . I've never done, I've never sort of thieved, you know what I mean like. If there's been an easy chance where I've been somewhere and I could pinch something I would, but . . . I've never sort of gone all out like, going out robbing to get money. I've sort of, like, borrowed it off people, you know what I mean. Like there's always my mum and my girlfriends, they've been my two main borrowers like. So I'd borrow off her like, and then I'd go and borrow off someone else to pay them back who I'd borrowed off . . . I just went round in a circle sort of thing. But I'd always seem to have enough money to, you know, get it like. You always sort of come up with something, manage to get it like. But when I worked on my habit, I was . . . something like £150 a week, you know something like that on heroin. But I was only getting £20-odd a week on the dole, and I'd be thinking, "How the hell am I getting the money?" like. You know what I mean? But you just don't really, you don't really know where you get it from. You just sort of seem to manage like.' (Jack, 22 years, Merseyside)

·If Jack did not know where his money was coming from, other people did. The daily routines of a heroin user often seem as if they are dictated by the beat of a metronome: getting up, hustling for money, buying heroin, smoking it, and then hustling for the next bag:

'Like you get up, you've gotta go out, get your money, get your smack, come back, use it . . . You're alright for ten minutes, go back out again, get money . . . you're turkeying after a couple of hours, can't get nothin', whatever, go back out again . . .' (Colin, 23 years, Manchester)

'When I . . . when you're hooked on it like, you don't want to go robbin' until you had a toot like, cos you can't run or nothin' if you got grabbed by the busies [police]. You wouldn't be able to leg away, and that like. So you'd have a toot to get your head together and then go out mooching . . .' (Eddie, 21 years, Merseyside)

'What was your typical day like?'
'You just, get your gear, smoke it, and then . . . wonder where you'll get your next bag from and watch a bit of telly, well that's it . . . that just makes you realize and you start thinking, "God, what am I gonna do for tonight now?" . . . So, like, you try and go out and get more money, and that like, so your whole day's just taken up . . . Go and do whatever you do for your money, buy your gear, get back, by then like . . . you smoke it . . . then tea-time comes around.' (Sharon, 21 years, Merseyside)

As a person's life begins to revolve around this rigorous timetable of events, various forms of thieving often simply become a matter of course. The most common forms of theft were probably shoplifting and burglary, although some people would become involved in more reckless forms of crime:

'What kinds of things did you get up to?'
'Everything. Snatches and everything. Like, I got stuck away for a theft. You know like the chippy up there, the woman and the fella were taking the money to the bank. I just ran past them and got the bag. Then, like, around Christmas time I just looked for briefcases in vans, and twice I copped for loads . . . £1300 and £800, just picked 'em up. Mind you, they were both unlocked, so it's their own

fault . . . But, everything that you can do, like petty things to snatches. Like robbing car radios – that's petty – but the next minute I'd do a till-snatch and that's not right, that's a bad thing to do. You get some gaol for that. But I didn't care. I didn't care.' (John, 19 years, Merseyside)

Not uncommonly, people who had never been in trouble with the law before started thieving, although what often distressed them most was that they had also stolen from their own families:

'I started robbin', robbed off my ma, took everything out of the house . . . and then, like, I just got right into robbin' and that like . . . Never even robbed in my life, you know, been in trouble, until I got into that . . . It was dragging me down. I was dragging my family down with me. As I say, I was robbin' of my mum and that, like I took the last tenner out of her purse and that when she left her bag . . . And she used to be able to leave it, her purse, in front of me on the mantle-piece, and it'd have all of her money, you know what I mean. And I wouldn't go near it or even think about robbin' off her. And you just do whatever . . . you know . . . Got to have that money when you're turkeying, and fuck everyone else like . . . Just a bad thing.' (Eddie, 21 years, Merseyside)

'Well everyone that I knew like, before they went on smack, they very seldom used to rob. They used to rob now and again, but not much . . . I think everybody robbed now and again like. But now they're robbing cos they've got to rob . . . they're robbing for the smack and before they weren't bothered. I've even known people who'd rob off their own families. I mean I couldn't do that, I'd rather go shoplifting, you know what I mean . . . In any case, my mum was looking after my little girl, and like robbing off her would've been like robbing off myself, you know, or robbing off my baby.' (Gail, 20 years, Merseyside)

'Yeh, I was into shoplifting and everything. I've even stole off my own, you know what I mean, the family . . . and they still stuck with me. They knew me before I went on heroin and what I was like, and my mum and dad must've thought . . .

"well, you know, he's not really like that, that's not him, he wouldn't do that." But I have done that, stole off my family and lied and that . . . You'll do anything, I mean anything, as long as you get that money.' (Paul, 24 years, Merseyside)

While listening to these recollections, it would be a mistake to think that they merely reflected an indiscriminate form of thieving, driven only by the compulsion of the attempt to avoid withdrawal – even though that is often how it is phrased, perhaps in an attempt to deny the responsibility for one's actions. Sharon, for example, conjured with a strange form of moral argument which, although she agreed that crime was wrong, allowed addicts to be excused from responsibility for their conduct because they were acting under a compulsion. In particular, she disagreed with the idea that people who robbed for heroin should be described as 'animals':

'They don't want to do the things, like, you know what I mean . . . people getting battered and that, just for £20 to pay for it. They don't want to do it. But it's just like you've got to do it. Cos if you're turkeying, you'll do *anything* for the money. So, like, these people who get called animals and all that like for robbing . . . you know, like, in the papers . . . they're not animals, it's just like they're doing something to feed their habit. They can't help it. So, like, I don't agree with what they say, that people are like animals cos they rob . . . it's not like that. If they weren't turkeying, they wouldn't even dream of it . . . Cos I know, I've been turkeying like, and things I've never even dreamt of doing in my life I've thought of doing . . . like, perhaps, grabbing someone's bag, just things like that . . . you know, coming out of a pub . . . and I would never even dreamt of doing something like that before. But now, like, you wouldn't stop at nothing.' (Sharon, 21 years, Merseyside)

However, this would again seem to imply a totally indiscriminate approach to crime. But Sharon knew from her own experience that thieving was so well integrated into the heroin economy that certain stolen articles are more acceptable than others. Indeed, where she lived – as in other parts of the country – it is not uncommon for dealers to accept stolen goods in direct exchange for heroin, without having to trade in these goods or 'fence' them for cash:

'Oh yes, I know what you mean now. Yeh, you can do that . . . like, say rob a jumper like and then give it to someone, and they'll say, "I'll give you four bags of smack." Is that what you mean?
'Yes.'
'Oh yeh, you can do that! That's what everyone does I think . . .' (Sharon, 21 years, Merseyside)

As Sharon, explained, there are also some kinds of theft which are not only more profitable, but which also require less skill and make for easier forms of exchange for cash:

'Some mug, like they go up and grab chains off girls' necks and all that like . . . In fact I think that's coming in more than what shoplifting is now . . . Like grabbing someone's bag, or the sovereign around their neck. It's much easier isn't it? All you're doing is just walking past them and grabbing it and getting off. I think that is going to come more like – bag snatching and purse snatching and all that. Because it's easier, and you're guaranteed to get like . . . well, with a sovereign you'll get more money than what you will if you go lifting in a shop wouldn't you? If someone come to you with a sovereign, like I'll say for thirty quid, you'd snatch it up wouldn't you? So like, I think that's what a lot of people are going for now.'

The awkward fact about property crime is that, viewed in purely economic terms, Sharon is quite right: there is a vigorous demand for stolen goods which enable people to purchase various commodities at much lower prices than they would otherwise be able to afford. Cheryl and her companions, for example, would sometimes go thieving with a 'shopping list' of articles for which people had placed orders. Of course, it was not always like that:

Question What did you do, just go straight into town and go shoplifting in the morning?

Cheryl	Oh no, most of't time I'd have money . . . anyway I couldn't go shoplifting unless I had smack.
Mother	Smack used to give her't confidence to go and do it.
Question	Did you go for anything in particular?
Cheryl	At one bit, we used to get all electrical gear . . .'
Mother	Anything! They'd come back wi' anything.
Cheryl	You get owt you can get your hands on, don't you? You can't be choosy can you?
Wendy	Yeh . . . [laughs] . . . 400 dimmer-switches from Woodwards' . . . [laughs] . . . Do you remember that?
Cheryl	Sometimes we'd go wi' a list of what people wanted . . . Used to get drills and whisky and salmon, coffee . . .
Wendy	She were more of a big shop-lifter, weren't you? And I were more petty me . . .

(Cheryl and Wendy, early 20s, South Yorkshire)

And then, always, the tall stories are brought out, about crimes inevitably committed by someone else, somewhere else, and maybe even on some other planet:

Wayne	I've known somebody to walk outside o' Curry's wi' a reet big trolley, and get a fridge-freezer . . .
Cheryl	Yeh.
Wayne	You know what I mean? White smock on . . . and just . . .
Cheryl	You know them trolleys, like what delivery men use and that? They took a fridge-freezer and an automatic washer . . . wi' white smocks on and all that, just like delivery men . . .
Wayne	I mean how can anyone have any cheek to do something like that? How can anyone have't bottle or't cheek?
Wendy	It's been done, though, hasn't it? Videos and . . .

Videos are among the favoured targets for thievese, of course, because of the ease with which they can be sold or 'fenced'. Although not always so easily as in the tall story of the 'video on an elastic band', passed on as allegedly the greatest 'scam' ever perpetrated in outer Manchester:

'Here I'll tell you a good one. There were these lads, three or four of 'em, had this video right? They'd nicked it, right, and . . . you're not gonna believe this, in fact I'm not sure I believe it my fucking self, but here you go . . . They had this video, just the one. And they'd go around the boozers, just the two of them like, and get chatting you know with some fella . . . Then, like, they'd bring up that they had this video, you know, wanted to get rid of it, was he interested for fifty quid, all that like . . . Now, if he said yeh – and people do, like, don't they? – they'd give him all this business about how they didn't have it with them right now, you know, but they could bring it round to his house. That way they'd get his address, like . . . and then say, "Oh hang on" . . ., and suddenly discover that they could hand it over there and then. Right? So, this fella goes off with his video, having paid them the hows-your-father, fifty quid like . . . pleased as punch, right. Little does he know that two days later, one of the other lads what he hasn't met, comes knocking on the door at his house, "Where's the video? My brother's video got nicked and I hear you've got it" – and this and that, putting the shits up this fella. Like, that he's gonna call the fucking cops and all the business. Right? Gets the video back, right, and then this is the bloody silly bit . . . and then the crafty buggers pull the same trick in another boozer with some other poor mug the day after . . . Have you ever heard anything like that? I mean it takes the bloody biscuit doesn't it? Smackheads, like . . . well I don't need to tell you that. But . . . you know, just one bloody video, like it was on an elastic band or something . . . a fucking boomerang, you know . . .' (Colin, 23 years, Manchester)

Whether or not this story is true is neither here nor there. Tall stories (and this is only one among many) serve an important function in the heroin world. They speak to the resourcefulness and inventiveness shown by people who, otherwise, describe themselves and their friends only as if driven by an uncontrollable compulsion. It is again necessary, then, to listen to the overlapping shifts of explanation and emphasis by which heroin users give an account of their actions and motives, sometimes describing themselves as powerless victims of pharmacology, at others painting a picture of life in which they emerge as decisive actors. At its lowest levels, the wheels of the heroin economy are oiled by this prolific economic activity – thieving, hustling, dealing – and to pretend that this is anything other than people exercising conscious choices between different forms of action would be to concede far too much to the pharmacological enslavements of the drug.

Sometimes, the tall story is told no doubt simply for the joy of telling it. Gail, for example, who was in receipt of a prescription for methadone maintenance disapproved of people abusing the system, but she nevertheless could not resist making a joke of it by recounting one of the more improbable stories circulating in Liverpool at the time:

'I don't agree with putting everyone on maintenance like, cos a lot of people are just using it. You know, like they take smack just once and go for a water test at the clinic and that . . . and that's it, like, to get you off the smack they give you a three weeks course. And they're just getting it for someone else. I've heard of people who's gone in there, they don't even use smack, they just use it for that day to get methadone to sell to other people, like . . . And oh, some of the things they do like! You know, lads who get an addict to pee in a bottle for them, and then going in the clinic like with the bottle stuck up their jumper and all that . . . and then hand that over as their own, you know what I mean, for the water test? And coming out with methadone, and they've never even seen smack! God, honest, the things that are going on, you wouldn't believe it.' (Gail, 20 years, Merseyside)

And you are not necessarily expected to believe it either, although it must be admitted that it is a good story. On other occasions, the tall story can also be read as a self-parody:

'Like, I've walked in shops, jumped over the till, grabbed the till . . . I could've got stuck away for years, you know what I mean. Done some things, like walked in a shop, just walked behind the counter and grabbed the money . . . Daft things like . . . Everyone knew who I was as well, it was just up the hill round here, a shop just round the corner from my mam's . . . like just walk in with a balaclava on your head, pull it down when you walk in the shop and . . . As if they wouldn't know who you was, like. The fella in the shop, he just turned around and said, "Oh, that's the lad who always comes in." You know what I mean? How can anyone be as stupid as that? I didn't care. That's the only way I can explain it like. I just didn't care.' (John, 19 years Merseyside)

Even so, John cared about some things. For example, he has never done a domestic burglary, and as he explains it this had to do with his strong feelings of loyalty to his mother:

'There's two things I've never done in my life, and I'm pretty made up. I've never like mugged anyone, you know mugged 'em, hit them and robbed their stuff. And I've never robbed a house . . . never, ever robbed a house. I wouldn't rob a house, no . . . that's, know what I mean, if our house got robbed and we woke up next morning. Here y'are, my ma's got the house to look nice you know after years like with her being on her tod and all that. And like, for somebody to walk in and rob that, rob everything she's got for their smack. No, like, if I caught anyone trying to rob our house I reckon I'd just kill them . . . Oh I would . . . I'd kill them or stab them to death. Just for them to walk in and rob our video, rob our telly, rob anything, the meters . . . just for them, like, I'd kill. I would . . . That's why I've never, ever robbed a house in my life. Never.'

Eddie offered a similar if somewhat less melodramatic version of the same moral distinction. Even though he confessed that he had stolen from his mother (just as John and so many others did) he nevertheless balked at committing a burglary on someone else's house:

'I started robbin', robbed off my ma . . . I've done shop-lifting and that like. But I've never robbed houses . . . like warehouses and things like that, yeh. But like, I knew my limit.. I couldn't rob a house, you know what I mean. Cos like, they're just the same class . . . Our house has been done like, and I just went right off my head . . .'

'Where was that, at your mother's?'

'Yeh . . . Just the thought of, like someone being in your house . . .' (Eddie, 21 years, Merseyside)

Heroin users so often describe their crimes as resulting from some form of compulsion, and yet it must be a very strange kind of compulsion. Allegedly, and on Eddie's own account, heroin obliterates all moral sensibility. But this is obviously not always true. Some moral hurdles must be higher than others.

On the game: ' . . . as long as I don't have to do it'

Just as thieving is not only an activity engaged in by heroin users, nor is prostitution, although it has been one of the traditional means by which both women and men have sometimes supported their habits. Female prostitution is, of course, undoubtedly more common than male prostitution, offering to women a more effective form of economic choice than that available to men. To describe prostitution as merely an economic choice will no doubt strike many people as quite scandalous; but that, nevertheless, is what it is. In Marsha Rosenbaum's book, *Women on Heroin*, which is the only serious study of female heroin users, prostitution emerges as undoubtedly a faster way of making money than any of the other forms of work available to women, whether legal or illegal.

Whether or not she becomes a prostitute, however, the very fact that a woman gets involved in heroin at all is often seen as a moral abomination. As Marsha Rosenbaum describes it, whereas a certain amount of glamour can come to be attached to the male addict, women who use heroin are readily defined as 'damaged goods'. So that young men who might themselves have been involved all manner of criminal activities, whether dealing or robbing, would express a certain amount of unease about a woman's involvement in the heroin scene:

'You know, it just doesn't seem right somehow. I don't like
to see girls getting involved. I mean, my girl hates the
smack, just hates it . . . she's taken it off me more than once,
and you know, flushed it down the lavatory and all that.
And that's alright . . . Well, you know, I didn't think so at
the time like, I screamed my head off at her and what have
you. But, no, I don't like to see a girl using smack. They do,
though.' (Colin, 23 years, Manchester)

It is hardly surprising, then, that prostitution was considered
to be completely off the map. This might be expressed as a
matter of sorrow:

'Yeh, there's lots of girls getting into it now. Some nice girls,
as well, some lovely looking girls. And now they're just
wasted on it . . . I know a few girls myself who are on the
game, just to supply their habit . . . It's a shame.' (Paul, 24
years, Merseyside)

But it could also be something to be regarded with contempt,
which rendered young women morally worthless. John, for
example, who did not have an exactly spotless record where
robbing and thieving were concerned, took the view that girls
who were prepared to 'do anything' to support their heroin
habits were 'not worth a carrot':

'It's bad when you see girls on it. Like, there's been some,
well, dead respectable girls . . . and now like, they're not
worth a carrot. Like, they're just bad girls, you know. They'd
do anything for it and all that, they're bad. There used to be
some who used to be like, brilliant to get on with and
everything. All dead nice looking. Down there, like, of a
night time now . . . there's about thirty girls every night.
They're worse than the lads now, girls . . .' (John, 19 years,
Merseyside)

We can contrast these scandalized reactions of young men
who had become involved in crime in order to sustain their
dependence on heroin with that of a woman who had turned
to prostitution for the same reason. Becoming a prostitute, as
she described it in an entirely matter-of-fact way, was not a

morally superior activity than thieving – it was simply one which she found more agreeable, when faced with a financial crisis as a result of her heroin addiction.

Like everything else, Julie was introduced to prostitution through friends, just as friends had introduced her to heroin, and would eventually teach her how to inject herself when her smoking habit became too expensive to maintain. She had been using heroin for not much more than six months, and she and her boyfriend were smoking more than a gram a day between them, and what savings they might have had were gone.

'It went on like that all through the summer . . . we were smoking an awful lot between us.'

'How were you getting the money.'

' . . .[laughs] . . . I started going out on the game . . .'

'How did you first start that? What was it like for someone who'd never done that before?'

'Hm, again that was people I'd got to know. I'd come to meet quite a few girls who were doing it, you know, they were friends . . . and blokes that my boyfriend was going about with, a lot of their women were on the game.'

'And were they heroin users too?'

'Hm, the girl, the particular girl that I first went out on the street with, she wasn't but her boyfriend was. And she was sort of supporting his habit. But she'd been on the game before, since she was about fifteen or sixteen or something like that. And it just seemed a quite easy way to get a lot of money. So I just started going out on the game.'

'Did you go on the streets, or in the clubs?'

'On the streets.' (Julie, 29 years, West Yorkshire)

The financial requirements of Julie's and her boyfriend's heroin habits were beginning to approach £600 to £700 per week at local prices, and the only way that she could even think of getting her hands on this kind of money was through prostitution. When she took this step, however, her boyfriend did not like to think that he was being kept by her and tried to maintain an independent form of income (eventually he was caught for shoplifting), but Julie must have been supplying most of their joint financial needs for some time. At first she was nervous, but quickly found that it was a very easy way to make money:

'What was it like the first few times?'

'I suppose I was quite nervous . . . yeh I was, I was really nervous. I got myself together and went out on the street anyway. The girl who went out, you know, to show me where all the girls stood and everything . . . she sort of genned me up on, you know, the patter of what to say to the punters and everything.'

'What do you have to say?'

'You just say, "Do you want business?" And if they say yes, they ask you how much, you tell them how much, and . . .'

'Is there a standard rate?'

'Yeh. Well, most of the girls, £10, that's to take them back to your house, but if they want you to strip off, an extra fiver. And if they want to kiss you and mess about as well, you know foreplay and that, that's an extra fiver. If they want more than sex, that's an extra fiver, or a tenner. You just . . . you can sus out how much you're going to get out of it. I mean you get as much as you can. Which can be quite a lot of money really . . .'

'How much? Give me an idea.'

'The first night I went out with this girl, I think I earned about £100 or something, and I thought well this is alright . . . I didn't keep it up all the time. But . . . well, if I go with say three or four, then I'm, you know, I've got say sixty, eighty pounds, or something like that. And that's enough. I can do that in about an hour and a half every night. So . . .'

'It's quick isn't it?'

'Quite a little business! If you're lucky . . . it just depends how much competition there is, you know, how many girls there are out and things like that. Sometimes there's half a dozen of us in a row, all standing there all coming down you know, desperate to take a punter so that they can get money for a £10 bag.'

Viewed from the outside, this seems a rather dismal way to

be going on, carrying with it all manner of social and moral disapproval. One way of describing the differences between crime and prostitution might be to say that whereas property crime externalizes the consequences of one's actions, causing injury to someone else – and we have seen how for some young men domestic burglary was out of the question because it did not quite 'externalize' their crime enough, and reminded them of their mother's homes – prostitution internalizes one's actions, causing self-injury. But this is not how Julie saw things. As far as she was concerned, crime was frightening because it involved a potential loss of control; whereas with prostitution she was in control. In fact, she even found that she quite liked it.

'No, I couldn't go shoplifting or anything like that, I'd be too frightened of getting caught. You know, you don't know what's going to happen . . . one slip and that's it. On the street, I know what I'm doing. I do what I want to and nothing else, sort of thing.'

'So, you don't really mind it?'

'Oh yeh, I don't mind at all . . . I meet the same women and the same blokes as well . . . you can have a chat with people, and that.'

'Do you only solicit those who you like the look of, or anybody?'

'Well . . . there are a lot I don't . . . er, I won't go with because I don't like the look of. But you know, I haven't . . . I don't find any of them repulsive or anything, they all turn out to be really nice blokes. You have the odd one or two who, you know, you've maybe been with them once but I don't like the way they are with me, then . . . you know, I'll not come back with them the next time I see them.'

'But most of them are quite . . .'

'Oh yeh, they're smashing, yeh.'

'Do you actually enjoy doing it then?'

'Yeh I do.'

Perhaps this comes too close to implying that Julie liked prostitution for its own sake, whereas in fact the sense of being in control was quite fundamental to her peace of mind. When all is said and done, this was for her an entirely rational activity. Its value to her was not meeting nice people, but obtaining sufficient money to supply her heroin habit:

'It's not something you hate doing, then; you quite like being with them?'

'I like doing it as long as I don't have to do it. You know, if I owe money for heroin and I've got to go out on the street to pay a debt, so that I can get some more . . . then I hate it. But if, you know, if I'm ahead which I find that I am all the time now, I'm okay for money, then . . . well, I'm going out, you know, and the money that I'm making's mine to do what I want with sort of thing. And that's okay.'

'And what do you do with it?'

' . . . [laughs] . . . Buy heroin!'

'Nothing else?'

'Not a lot else, no.'

Climbing Back:
'Coming Off' and 'Staying Off'

There comes a time when a heroin user discovers the motivation, for whatever reason, to try to 'come off' the drug. It might be simply that someone has become tired of the heroin lifestyle, or that they are afraid they will do themselves an injury if they do not stop. A change of friends can be an important consideration, or the damage which their heroin use is doing to their families might weigh heavily on their minds. A variety of reasons are given for deciding freely to 'come off' heroin: a fear of being caught for shoplifting or other crimes; a new boyfriend who does not use drugs; in order to set an example to one's spouse who is also a user. Sometimes it is an enforced decision, maybe because the local supply of heroin has been disrupted. Or, not uncommonly, it is because a heroin user is facing a court appearance – either for the possession of drugs, or for theft – in which case they might hope that it will influence the decision of the court if they are seen to be making an effort to change their lifestyle. A court appearance which has resulted in a probation order or a deferred sentence can also concentrate the mind wonderfully, if someone feels that this is their 'last chance' and that a prison sentence will inevitably follow if their heroin use continues. Nevertheless, it is probably true to say that all self-motivated attempts to 'come off' heroin take place within one form or another of subtle compulsion: from family, friends, social workers or the cost-benefit calculations of falling foul of the law.

The ways in which people try to 'come off' heroin also vary considerably. Some people rely on the help of professionals, either through their family doctor or by attending a local drug clinic where one is available, in which case they might undergo a methadone-reduction programme designed to wean them off the drug. This might be done either as an out-patient or as an in-patient, and there are also a variety of residential facilities such as rehabilitation centres and the 'concept houses' – although residential therapy is clearly not an option for people with family responsibilities, and certainly not for single parents. The pattern of available services suffers from a widespread local and regional variation, moreover, leading sometimes to disappointment when a person refers themselves to a local clinic hoping to receive one form of help (maybe methadone maintenance) only to find that it is not a form of help that it locally available – a disappointment which can either lead to someone continuing to use heroin, or deciding to improvise their own self-help means of 'coming off'. Many people, in fact, simply prefer to go it alone, either by just sitting it out at home while they go through the period of withdrawal, or by taking themselves off for a holiday to an area where they will not be able to obtain heroin, thereby removing themselves from the temptation to have 'a little toot' with their friends in order to relieve the withdrawal symptoms.

And if the motives and methods differ, then so does the pace at which people try to 'come off' heroin. For some it is a once-and-for-all process, of simply going through withdrawal and getting it over with in a matter of days. Others attempt to do it over a period of weeks or even months, by a series of gradual steps: first from injecting to smoking, maybe, then from smoking heroin to methadone maintenance, and eventually to a methadone-reduction course. Although, whether someone can do it this way will again depend on the availability of the right kind of specialist services in their locality. There are large controversies among medical practititioners, for example, particularly about whether methadone should be prescribed on a maintenance basis – local medical policy will therefore limit the choices which people can make about how to approach the question of 'coming off' heroin.

As someone does approach the decision to 'come off', the question of withdrawal symptoms looms large in their minds. In all probability, they will already have experienced withdrawal sickness at one time or another, if only at times of scarcity when they have been unable to obtain heroin to feed their habit. Even so, the decision to 'come off' is a different matter altogether, because it is no longer a question of racing around the area in order to find a 'bag' somewhere, which might then be shared with one's friends who are also 'turkeying', affording a little 'toot' or a 'taste' to take the edge off withdrawal. To contemplate 'coming off' is both a matter of resolving to see it through to the end, as well as facing an essential loneliness without either the excitement of the hunt or the companionship of fellow users.

What heroin users also say is that 'coming off' is one thing, but that 'staying off' is the real problem. The discomfort experienced when withdrawing from heroin is real, but it is nevertheless vastly exaggerated in many of the highly self-dramatized accounts of 'cold turkey'. It is more like a bad dose of influenza – with aches and pains, a runny nose and eyes, incessant yawning, sleeplessness, goose pimples, vomiting and diarrhoea – complicated by a craving for the drug. The worst is over in no more than three or four days, although it might be as long as ten days or a fortnight until someone begins to feel completely right in themselves again. Then, there begins a more protracted struggle to 'stay off' heroin, which will involve establishing new forms of daily routine to replace the rigorous daily timetable of sustaining a heroin habit, and maybe also breaking contact with old friends and users. 'Coming off' heroin and 'staying off' is not easy. But it can be done.

Cold turkey: 'I were dying . . . well I weren't, but . . .'

When someone first uses heroin, as we have seen, the accounts which are given of the drug's pleasurable effects often seem vague and incoherent. Some people say that its effects creep upon you slowly, while others say that it gives them an urgent bodily charge. Some describe it as relaxing, while others enjoy it as a 'buzz' or a 'hit'. And so on.

There is a very similar problem in unravelling the experience of withdrawal, which often seems very difficult for heroin users to put across, and which is also described in different terms by different people. This might be because the experience of withdrawal does actually vary for different people, with some suffering more severe physiological reactions than others. Or it might be because people had been accustomed to using different quantities of heroin daily, or had been using the drug for varying lengths of time. The experiences of withdrawal are also sometimes thought to be very different according to whether someone is smoking heroin or injecting it, with those who inject finding it more difficult because of what they describe as a 'needle fixation'. Or these variations could be because people use heroin for different reasons – whether to enjoy the 'hit', or to cushion themselves from painful emotions – so that withdrawal means different things to them. But what is certain is that the common description of 'cold turkey' as a horrifying experience that is beyond the extremities of ordinary understandings of human pain, is not always shared by heroin users who have gone through the experience of withdrawal.

> ' . . . the turkey's not too bad, you know, you can still keep your head sort of together, and like you still know what's going on, you know what I mean. I mean you hear of people who don't know where the fuck they were, and they don't know what was going on. But like I've always sort of . . . I've known what's going on, but it's just unbearable the feeling that you get like . . . I mean it's dead hard to explain what a turkey is.' (Colin, 23 years, Manchester)

This low-key description of withdrawal is in fact quite typical. It is not that the discomfort is denied, or even felt to be occasionally unbearable, but it is something that has to be done and can be done. Sometimes, as people struggle to convey a sense of what the experience is like, there is an apparent level of contradiction. For example:

'Is it as bad as they make out?'

'No, I don't think so. It's bad, really, but you can't explain it like. It's hard to explain what a turkey is, like . . . A lot of people say this happens and that happens, but when I done my turkey it wasn't as bad as I was expecting. But it was bad, if you know what I mean . . . It was unbearable, like, but it wasn't as bad as I was expecting.' (Eddie, 21 years, Merseyside)

The veiled uncertainty in Eddie's description was often repeated. Cheryl, who was sometimes given to highly drama-tized accounts of her experiences with heroin, offered a much more straightforward account of the difficulties of withdrawal. Although the contradictions still showed through:

'How many times have I turkeyed? I went in't nick once and got off my turkey didn't I? I went to prison, and were in for four week and got off my turkey didn't I?'

'What do you reckon about withdrawals then?'

'Well, it's hardest thing in my life that I've ever had to go through. Hardest thing like, I feel reet sorry for people now me . . . I still do off methadone, I still withdraw off methadone. Cos like it's just same as heroin isn't it? . . . Well, it in't but . . . One time he cut me down too much, and I couldn't do it, you know I couldn't manage wi' what he were geeing me . . . and I were dying . . . Well, I weren't, but . . .' (Cheryl, 20 years, South Yorkshire)

Each of these accounts is plagued by ambiguity, reflecting what would seem to be an inherent difficulty in describing the internal states associated both with the effects of heroin and also withdrawal from it. So that faced with these difficulties, the heroin user will sometimes resort to the sterotype of the horrors of 'cold turkey', although even then they will cover their tracks by an explicit disclaimer: 'I were dying, well I weren't, but . . .'; 'It was unbearable, like, but it wasn't as bad as I was expecting'; 'the turkey's not too bad . . . but it's just unbearable like . . . I mean it's dead hard to explain'.

Another way in which people describe the effects of withdrawal, once more conflicting with the common stereotype, is to say that the real difficulties are not bodily but 'psychological' and 'in your head'.

> 'So apart from those times when you've been off it for a couple of months, have you ever tried coming off again?'
> 'Er, quite a few times I've come off it for like seven days; I haven't touched it for seven days, but gone back on it. It's not the actual coming off, you know this thing you hear, "cold turkey" and all that . . . That's, most of it's in your head, you know, mental, memory sort of thing . . . I think people get the wrong ideas.' (Paul, 24 years, Merseyside)

In Sharon's experience, moreover, there was sometimes a bewildering state of feeling when according to everything that you knew about heroin you should be withdrawing, although in fact the symptoms failed to appear on cue. As she described it, once more with the characteristic ambiguities fully in evidence, there were a number of different levels of experience which included not only the physical symptoms of withdrawing, but also their 'psychological' components together with the anxiety about whether you were going to be able to get the next bag:

> 'As soon as you wake up, it's like a ton of bricks coming down like, "Where am I going to get my money from today?" But like, when you think about it now, most of it is psychological . . . Like you wake up and you think, "I should be turkeying" and that, but you're not turkeying . . . "What's going on? I'm not turkeying" . . . Then all of a sudden you've got the sweats, you're shaking . . . I wouldn't say, like, you can just forget about it, going for a walk, it's not like that. I'm saying like, you wake up in the morning . . . like I think everyone gets up in a morning and they start turkeying, it's natural isn't it? But you wake up and you're feeling alright, and you think, "I should be turkeying" . . . I think a lot of it's in your head . . . But I wouldn't say it was easy.' (Sharon, 21 years, Merseyside)

Getting help: 'Come back in six weeks'

From the experiences of these people, there would seem to be no reason for a heroin user to be excessively fearful of withdrawal. It is not a pleasant experience, but nor is it the end of the world. As Paul described the episodes of withdrawal that he had known, it was simply a question of settling down to go through a bad patch for a few days:

'As I say, you're not really . . . you're only . . . your first four days are pretty bad, you know, you get the flu symptoms, you sweat, and you can't sleep for the first three or four nights, you get diarrhoea, your legs are weak . . . But then, after that, the four days, five days, you're on the up then.' (Paul, 24 years, Merseyside)

As Paul understood it, 'coming off' was not the problem. The real difficulty was 'staying off', especially when heroin was still available in the area in which you lived. This was echoed elsewhere:

'Staying off's the hard part. Coming off? It's nowt really, there's not much to it like. There's a few of us round here, who've all been on smack, got sick of it. And you get nowt over there at the clinic, there's no methadone or what have you. So, you know, we just do it on us own like. It's bad for a few days, but . . . Get stocked up with, you know, comics and magazines, chocolate and pop and that. Go to bed, and just sit it out. That's all there is to it. Like I say, there's a few of us done it, so we know what the crack is . . . you know, we can help each other out and that. There's a lad only the other week, he'd got sick of it, so we said "Here you are . . .", showed him the ropes. He's off it now, like . . . Then there's, er, some leaflets and that you can get . . . You know, like telling you that lasses who are in't family way shouldn't do it on their own, you know, should take it more steady with a doctor's advice and that. But I didn't bother with doctors. I mean, they're all right, but there's nothing they can do really. You can get methadone, you know, on one of those reduction courses . . . But we didn't see no point. Just do it on us own. In fact, from what I've heard that methadone's worse to get off than the smack . . . so, we just do it on us own. That's it.' (Ronnie, 21 years, Manchester)

This is probably the best kind of level-headed advice that can be given to a heroin user who wishes to come off, and although specialist opinion is divided about whether it is better for a pregnant woman to attempt withdrawal or continue to use heroin for the duration of the pregnancy, there are certainly risks to the foetus if she tries to go through withdrawal too rapidly on her own in this way. Methadone, moreover, might well be more harmful to the foetus than heroin. Of course, not everyone will have either the courage to attempt such self-help remedies, nor access to a supportive network of experienced ex-users who can offer advice and encouragement. Nevertheless, 'coming off' on your own is quite clearly an achievable objective.

Even so, many people continue to fear withdrawal, largely because they remain trapped in the mythologies of heroin's demonic powers of enslavement and the excruciating agonies of 'cold turkey'. What is more, these mythologies can offer yet another form of subterfuge by which heroin users convince themselves (and others) that they must continue to take the drug and cannot contemplate 'coming off'. When, however, someone has conquered these fears and decided to take action on a heroin problem, or decided that the consequences of not taking any action would be even worse than suffering withdrawal, they may have only taken the first step in what might prove to be a long and painful process of climbing back.

The decision to 'come off' can often be taken quite suddenly, however, although a person's motivation might then be correspondingly frail if it does not meet with a speedy and adequate response from their friends, family or professional helpers. Long waiting lists at over-stretched clinics and other stumbling blocks in gaining access to treatment can easily dent such frail motivations. June, for example, was a young woman in her early twenties who had developed a daily heroin habit after about six months of use. Her motivation to do something about this was triggered when a former boyfriend who had been working abroad, and of whom she had been very fond,

wrote to her to say that he was coming home. He was due
home in a month's time and June decided to stop using heroin
before his return, and took herself off to see her family doctor.

'He was very nice, I suppose . . . but he said he didn't know
how to treat a heroin addict, and all that, and that I had to
go to a clinic . . . that he'd give me an appointment for the
clinic, and that was all he could do.'
'So what happened at the clinic?'
'Well, I never went. The appointment was for six weeks,
you see, and Ian was coming home in a month. So it wasn't
a lot of use . . . Come back in six weeks, you know. I was
too embarrassed to explain to the doctor. But, anyway, he
didn't know what else to do. He made that clear.'
'So what did you do?'
'I just went home and cried . . . then went out, saw a
friend, had a toot with her like, and that was it . . . just
carried on.' (June, 22 years, Manchester)

Not everyone was quite as understanding of the doctor's
dilemma, however, as June appears to have been:

'After I'd been to court and that, and I realized I'd be going
away again if . . . you know . . . I went to the doctor for
help and that, but I got no joy. He just kept giving me
fucking tablets, pain-killers and all that, and they were doing
me no good like. And I said to him, "Give me some
methadone". You know, if I don't get off the gear I'll be
going to prison and all that. And he went, "No". If you want
to get methadone, you have to go to a clinic and get it
properly. You know what I mean, the doctors are a load of
shit, they don't want to know you . . . That's probably half
the reason, like, they don't know how to take it, what to do
or nothin'. They're fucking rubbish. So like, he give me a
letter and referred me to that clinic and that, and I got my
methadone in the end . . . and felt better for it. Always get a
bath and that, you know every day . . . before I was dead
scruffy.' (Gavin, 22 years, Merseyside)

Julie also encountered delays when she first tried to obtain
treatment. She had only been using heroin for maybe three

months at this point in time, but she had realized that her savings were fast disappearing and that she needed to do something about her problem.

> And I went to the doctor, told him that I had a problem . . . you know, that I was taking heroin, that I was taking it every day and that if I didn't take it I felt really bad. And this doctor said that, in however many years of practising as a doctor he'd never come across heroin use, that he didn't know how to deal with it, etcetera. So, the result of this was that about three weeks later I got an appointment card to go and see a Dr Quincey at the clinic, and the appointment was about three weeks later again . . . So that was a gap of six weeks between seeing the doctor and this appointment to see Dr Quincey the psychiatrist at Trent House . . . that's where the clinic was. And the day that I was supposed to go to Trent House clinic, I woke up, I didn't have any heroin, I felt dreadful. I'd no money to get to Trent House, I didn't know where it was, and I just didn't go. You know, that's it . . . I didn't get to that appointment to see Dr Quincey, and I just let things slide as you do.' (Julie, 29 years, West Yorkshire)

In fact, Julie did not just let things slide. Her heroin use continued to escalate, and shortly after this she turned to prostitution in order to support her habit.

David, on the other hand, was a young man from Liverpool who did manage to sustain his motivation until the time of a clinic appointment, whereupon he was given a routine urine-analysis and told to come back in four days' time. He failed to meet this second appointment, however, and phoned the clinic on the following day to ask if he could be seen after the weekend. Colin was told that it was clinic policy that if you failed an appointment, then you went to the back of the queue, which would have involved him waiting for another month. Whereupon, he took himself off to see his family doctor immediately:

> 'He told me he couldn't do nothing for me, cos now I was under the clinic like. I got really mad, shouting at him and all

that, and we had a bad argument me and the doctor. I
remember, I pulled this money out of my pocket and waved
it at him . . . like, "Look, I could go and buy smack now,
like, but I don't want it, I want some methadone to help me
get off." I wanted to get off it like. When he got it into my
head that he couldn't do nothin' for me, and that I had to
wait another month like . . . well, I thought, "Fuck it, I'll do
it on my own", like. And I did, and I've never bothered with
clinics or nothin' since . . .' (David, 22 years, Merseyside)

David's troubles, however, were not yet over. The strategy
which he devised was to take himself off on a holiday, away
from the area in which heroin was freely available to him, and
to attempt withdrawal in that way. So, armed with a supply of
pain-killers, he went off to Somerset near to where one of his
former friends now lived. On arrival, however, he found that
his mate who had also been a heroin user had got back into
heroin again. So, back to Liverpool. Next, David thought that
he would try the Isle of Man where one of his cousins had a
job, and this proved to be more successful.

'I was in the Isle of Man for six weeks, and I was off the
smack for all of that time like. Feeling really good with
myself, you know . . . and I could've had a job, painting
guest houses and that, but I had to come back to Court . . .
You know, I'd got caught for possession of heroin like. And I
said, I'll go to Court and come back over, cos they'd offered
me a job. But because I went to the Isle of Man . . . they
adjourned the Court case for reports . . . and he turned
round, the magistrate, and said to me – because I went to the
Isle of Man, you know what I mean, there's conditions to my
bail – you know, that I have to reside at my mam's house,
and that I had to sign on at the police station every night.
Honest to God, I couldn't believe it . . . how stupid can you
get? So I couldn't go back to the Isle of Man. And then, well
you know the rest like . . . within like two weeks I was back
on the gear again.'

Faced with these constant difficulties of obtaining adequate
help, or even a sympathetic response to their own efforts to

help themselves, heroin users will often become trapped within a recurring cycle of abstinence and relapse, so that families and friends will sometimes try to take things into their own hands. John had been referred to a local clinic, for example, hoping to receive methadone. But when this was not forthcoming, he continued using heroin, at the same time entering onto a reckless spiral of robbing and thieving to finance his habit. Fitful attempts to 'come off' always seemed to end with him going back to his heroin-using friends, until eventually his family tried to imprison him in the house:

'All I done was went down there, the clinic like, and he said, "Are you still taking it?" . . . "Yeh" . . . "Okay just try and get off it" . . . Do you know, he give me nothin'. And I was in the waiting room for three hours, walked in and sat down for a minute, and that was it. So I just said to my doctor I'm not going no more. But he said I'd better, it was the best thing like. And my ma was on at me . . .'

'Was that the local clinic, or . . .'

'No, the other one. It's last . . . I remember I went there one time, smacked up, and he just looked at me and said, "Are you taking it?" He didn't even know I was on it. Just last. Just didn't even know I was on it. I just said, em, "No, I'm not taking it" like, to see what they'd say. And he said, "Oh that's very good, ta-ra, see you next month." So I never bothered going again. Even my brother turned round and said to my mum, "It's not going to do him no good." And then they tried to lock me in the house. But I just got desperate and jumped out the window, and ran away for some smack.'

'What, your brother locked you in the house?'

'Yeh, and my mum. Every time I'd head for the door, someone'd put the bolts on. And before I could open it, they'd shut the door. It was terrible. So like, I jumped out the window . . . tried to run away. But I was that weak, I couldn't run. I walked, and my mum ran after me . . . I didn't know what I was doing.'

'How long did that go on for?'

'Oh it seemed like ages . . . And then my brothers had the baseball bats on me once'

'Did they?'

'I'd pawned my ma's sovereigns, you see . . . you know, to buy smack . . . and my two brothers walked in the bedroom, dragged me out of bed, and they knew where I'd put my gear that night and grabbed my gear, and one o' them threw it down the toilet . . . I started shouting at everybody, "What are you doing?" and all that. And one hit me on the knee with a baseball bat and I fell on the bed. And one of them grabs hold of my hair, like they were just going batter me, see, "Where's my ma's sovereigns?" and all that. And my ma walked in, and she'd found the pawn tickets like, and she'd got them out herself. And she just walked in and said, "Here y'are look, I've got them, I must've left 'em somewhere . . ." And she never even walked up to me, or asked me nothin'. She just said, "Here you are, I must have forgotten where they were" and just walked away. I felt last. It was worse than her telling me off, you know with her not saying nothin' . . .'

'Some people get thrown out by their parents.'

'Oh I've been thrown out . . . but she's always took me back. Always. Even when I got stuck away . . .'

'Was that for possession?'

'Robbing . . . But it had got as I didn't care. Like, I wanted to go to Risley. Just wanted to get off . . . just get off it.' (John, 19 years, Merseyside)

And John did then get off it, although it was in the cold comfort of a prison cell. His mother's tortured loyalties could be set to rest, at least for a time. Indeed, amidst the constant struggle between abstinence and relapse which can bring such frightful difficulties into people's lives, a gaol sentence might sometimes even seem like a blessing.

Needles again: 'You have two different addictions'

People's initial motivations to 'come off' heroin often seemed to founder amidst the complexities and inadequacies of overstretched treatment resources. Sometimes, of course, these motivations might not have been entirely sound, so that it would be wrong always to place the entire blame with the inadequacies of the organized systems of practical help. Even so, it is a disturbing feature of the accounts which heroin users and ex-users give of their experiences in trying to secure assistance that they often felt that they were met with what they perceived as a mixture of indifference, incompetence and sometimes even a malevolently punitive attitude.

Wherever one might wish to strike the balance, however, the outcome of these unhappy exchanges was that heroin users and their families were often thrust back onto their own resources in trying to combat the problems in their lives. This was the experience of Linda and Brian in South Yorkshire who, for eighteen months from the time when they had first realised that they had a problem with heroin, found it necessary to struggle on with a series of improvised remedies until they were finally able to secure what they could recognize as an effective response to their troubles. In their eyes, the only way that they could begin to come to terms with heroin was to receive a prescription for methadone. Their difficulties were complicated by the fact that they were injecting heroin, rather than smoking it, and when they attempted to achieve a withdrawal from heroin they found that giving up the needle was more difficult than giving up heroin – something which is commonly reported by heroin users who inject. Their efforts to overcome this 'needle fixation', in which Linda took the lead, were shaped within a labyrinth of conflicting emotions, full of twists and turns, unforeseen happenings and what must have been some pretty dreadful days and nights. Indeed, their route to a methadone prescription – which was ultimately successful, although again under quite unforeseen circumstances – was tortuous and haphazard in the extreme: a grim testimony to the inadequacies of our response to the new heroin problem.

It will be remembered that Linda and Brian had injected heroin on a regular basis for six months, when their supply was interrupted because of a blizzard in the Pennine hills, whereupon they discovered that they had become addicted and that they suffered from withdrawal sickness when they did not use the drug. Shocked by this eventuality, and somewhat unusually, they immediately consulted a doctor:

Brian   We went to us doctor, like, and't first week he gi'n us some physeptone, didn't he?

Linda   It were alright that, it seemed to sort us out . . . well not at first, but after a few days like.

Brian   And then we went back week after, and he stopped us . . . He'd phoned up someone, some specialist somewhere, who'd told him to stop. Like, "We've got to get yer off it." And from then on he'd only gee us like valium, and . . . that's no good at all, there's nowt in that. Not for heroin, anyway. There's only methadone or physeptone, which is same, there's only them that help like. And it took us from that day about eighteen months . . .

Linda   We told him we wanted to see Dr Smith . . . We'd heard about him from friends, and they said he were alright. You know, he'd given 'em methadone and that, and they'd been using heroin, and they were alright now.

Brian   Yeh. We'd heard about this fella, from us mates, like, who were at th'hospital and who did prescribe. And we tried to get to see 'im. But they said we couldn't see 'im, or nowt.

Question When was that?

Brian   That were . . . more than two year ago now. Yeh, two years. Like, as I said, it took us eighteen month to get to see him, Dr. Smith.

They had discovered methadone as the balm for their difficulty, though this was then promptly removed. Now unable to obtain a referral for whatever reason, to the psychiatrist whom they wished to see, Linda and Brian continued to use heroin. They were buying no more than a gram every fortnight, if that, when their social security giro arrived and eking out that small amount as best they could – in such a vivid contrast to those other heroin users whom we have encountered who were 'blasting' sometimes up to a gram per day. But even though they were using only a small amount of heroin, as they understood it their main problem was a dependence on the needle. They would no doubt have used more heroin if they had been able to afford it, but neither of them was prepared to turn to crime in order to support their habits, and they were desperately afraid of withdrawal sickness. Both of them were at that time still injecting, and becoming dispirited about their ability to do anything about their problem. What were they to do?

Describing how in her view it was only 'love' that had helped them to pull through, it was Linda who took the next step:

Linda   There's only one thing that gets yer off it, and that's love . . . Honestly, there's nothing else.
Brian   You've got to love somebody.
Linda   Cos that's how I got off't needle, like cos he lost his faith . . . He were reet spiritual at one time, well he is now, but lost it.
Brian   I just says to her, I remember one day, I said 'Look we've had it us' . . . I says, we're here for ever.
Linda   Never gonna get off it.
Brian   And then, like, she goes, 'Oh I'll bloody show you.' And then she never had a fix since . . .
Linda   This were before we got to see Dr Smith, this . . .
Brian   Yeh . . . months before; it must've been nine months before we saw him . . . Oh no, more. And we were still hitting it up like, and then Linda just stopped and started dragoning it, then like. I didn't know how she did it me . . .

In truth, she did it very slowly and painfully. Linda found that when she stopped using the needle, even though she continued to smoke heroin, she started to suffer from terrible dreams:

Linda   It's like nightmares, horrific nightmares, like . . . shooting . . .
Brian   Shooting your mother.
Linda   Killing people.
Brian   Yeh, killing your mates and that . . .
Linda   It's really real, and you wake up and . . . There's no

amount of heroin will tek that off. No amount . . .
Like we hadn't got much anyway, we never got much
like . . . but in my eyes no amount of heroin'd tek
withdrawal of the needle off. Only a needle'd tek
withdrawal off needle off . . .

It is not at all clear just how much heroin Linda and Brian
had been using, but it cannot have been a great deal, so that it
might have been that when she turned to smoking she was
simply taking insufficient of the drug to avoid withdrawal.
Linda was convinced, however, that her difficulties came from
the fact that she was no longer using the needle. As well as the
bad dreams, she was suffering from stomach pains, and in
order to ride through these difficulties what Linda did was to
withdraw herself slowly from what she understood as a
'needle fixation' by occasionally injecting a tiny amount of
heroin on an increasingly irregular basis:

Linda Like what I did at first, like, I went for a few days and
then . . . cos you get a feeling inside you, oh it's
terrible, it's like . . .
Brian Like an empty . . .
Linda Like there's something missing, like your stomach's
not there . . . And like, oh, it can crack you up can't
it? So, I'd have just a little bit of heroin in't needle . . .
cos it were for't needle I were having it, you know,
not for't heroin . . . and just have it in't works and
have it . . . And it'd go straight to my stomach, and
it'd take effect of needle off then . . .
Brian For a couple of more days like.
Linda So I'd go longer then, till . . . I kept doing that till I
went for, like, two weeks, then I'd have a little bit
more in't needle . . . a month, and so on, and so
on . . . And I got off it . . .
Brian That's how she did it like.

What we have here is two people, in the absence of any other
effective form of help, having to improvise both a course of
self-treatment and also a theory of addiction. Linda and Brian

were satisfied from their own experience, for example, that heroin was no more habit-forming than tobacco. The real difficulty in their eyes was overcoming their dependence on the needle.

Linda   Well, you see, it's bad when you use needle. Because you have two different addictions . . . So, it's the needle what you're withdrawing off . . . If you can get off needle, you can crack it wi' anything. That's where it's hardest . . . smoking, like, smoking . . . we can get off smoking can't we?

Brian   Yeh it's easy, it's easy smoking.

Linda   It's just an habit.

Brian   It's like a cig . . . not even as bad as smoking a fag, smoking henry like . . . There's only the actual rituals of doing it, the silver paper and all that. Like I started smoking it after Linda did, I started having bits and bobs like, but my main load were . . . you know I were still hitting it up.

Whether or not professional opinion would agree with this view is neither here nor there. The professional community, for the time being, had washed its hands of their difficulties. No doubt if Brian had been prepared to get himself caught for shoplifting, he might have found a probation officer who would have been able to oil the wheels of the system. As things stood, however, and for whatever reason, Linda and Brian were unable to gain access to local treatment facilities, having been fobbed off with minor tranquillisers by their family doctor. It is possible to argue, no doubt, that Linda was simply prolonging the agony by going through this rigmarole of injecting herself with a tiny dose of heroin once a week, once a fortnight, and then once a month until she stopped. Maybe she would have been better advised to go through a swift period of immediate withdrawal. But, of course, no-one was offering her advice. In any case, her experience and then that of Brian when he eventually stopped injecting, was that the nightmares and the other problems which they identified as originating with the needle carried on for much longer than the symptoms of heroin withdrawal. And so their trial continued:

Brian Like the dreams . . .

Linda The cold, too, you're really freezing. Then they say heroin's supposed to warm you up. But like, no way if you're coming off at needle. No chance if you've got nowt to take needle off, cos like I didn't have anything, I just went through it.

Brian She went through it, and I were still . . . she still saw me doing it, you know fixing like, and she . . .

Linda I had to, else he wouldn't . . . he'd never . . .

Brian I'd have never got off fixing like.

Linda You know he thought we were stuck . . . so I just stopped it like . . . Even now, if I see somebody wi' a needle, ooh . . . I go like that wi't stomach pain, and I have to go to't toilet, diarrhoea . . . and that's after fifteen month . . . goose pimples all over.

Brian But she did it . . . our Linda did it.

As time wore on, they tried to cut down on the level of their heroin use, even though this had never been much to start with. This was not only a matter of choice, however, it was also a question of financial necessity. They had developed a pattern of use in which they would frequently suffer withdrawal symptoms, using heroin sparingly to take the edge off the symptoms. They would also occasionally be given a small 'hit' by heroin-using friends who came to visit them. There were no doubt elements of subterfuge and self-deception in their responses, by which they convinced themselves that they must continue to use heroin, even in this haphazard and unhappy fashion. Although, increasingly, they were coming to feel that their problem might not be with heroin at all, but with the needle. Along the way of their dreadful odyssey, in fact, Linda and Brian later discovered a somewhat better remedy for their difficulties than a sparing use of heroin, in the form of the illicit trade in methadone:

Brian We got sick of it in't end. Really sick of it. But doctor wouldn't have nowt to do wi' us, for months like.

Linda There's nowt'll take it off . . . So in't end, there were linctus weren't there? But that were scarce.

Brian Yeh, there weren't a lot around like . . . but when

you could get it, it were cheaper than smack.

Linda What we used to try and do was to try and get a bottle from somewhere, so that we didn't have to have heroin.

Brian Yeh, rather than buy smack . . . rather than go and buy a quarter of a gram for twenty quid, we could go and buy a bottle o' linctus for twenty quid and that'd last us for two weeks, wouldn't it?

Linda Yeh, and then try and do't same again.

Brian But it were impossible, there weren't enough supply . . . But like, it were better to have that than to have smack, cos like all we needed were a little cap of linctus and that were it . . . for a fortnight.

Linda It were like gold, weren't it?

At this point, they might well have been digging an even deeper hole for themselves, because it is a common view that methadone is much more difficult to withdraw from than heroin itself. So that when the supply of illicit methadone linctus occasionally dried up, as it did, they would find their limited heroin intake even more inadequate to the task of staving off the symptoms of withdrawal.

And so they struggled on, for eighteen months in all, cobbling together one stop-gap measure after another. When they eventually succeeded in obtaining the psychiatric referral which they had sought throughout this time, it came from a most surprising source. Because it did not come through medical channels, but by the decision of a Magistrate's Court:

Linda So in't end, he had to grass his self up at Court, to get to see 'im. Didn't you?

Brian Aye. I stood up in Court, it were a driving offence like. And they said, 'Why did you use this car?' and all that. I'd borrowed this lad's car, and it weren't taxed or insured or nowt like. I says, 'I used it to get heroin' like.

Linda He says, 'I'm an heroin addict!'

Brian They were all . . . 'Aargh!' . . . They were all shocked like. 'We'd better go in't back here', like. So they all went out for half an hour, and they come back and said, 'Psychiatric reports' like, and we got to see Dr Smith . . . that way . . . And what he did wi' us, cos we had to go back in Court following week, we went to see 'im on't next day, and day after that we got us supply of methadone, didn't we? And we've never looked back from then. From that day we never touched nowt.

Marking time on methadone: 'You don't need to rob'

Of course, in saying that from the day that he received methadone he stopped using drugs, Brian is not strictly correct. He may not have used heroin anymore, but he did nevertheless use methadone. One might even say, and some would say, that he simply swapped one addiction for another. Indeed, Brian and Linda said it themselves:

Linda Cos you get addicted to it, you know like . . .
Brian That's the idea isn't it?'
Linda Like, you get off heroin, then you get addicted to linctus.
Brian The idea is to get hooked on it.
Linda . . . You could do with something to help you get off that, though . . . to get off methadone.
Brian There's nowt to help you get off that, though, that's trouble.
Linda You've got to do it yourself, that.
Brian You've got to like, cut yersen down and just . . . stop tekking it. Look, I'm not using nearly as much as I used to. I've got all this left in't bottle . . . [waves the bottle] . . . and I see 'im again tomorrow. That's it . . . there's no-one else can do it. You've got to do it yersen.

A large debate hangs over the question of prescribing methadone (also known as physeptone) on a 'maintenance' basis as a substitute for heroin. It removes the user's craving for heroin, but it also replaces one form of drug dependence for another, and some medical practitioners will refuse to prescribe methadone except as part of a strict reduction programme during which a person's methadone intake is progressively reduced until they are eventually abstinent. It is the view of those medical practitioners who hold to an abstinence model of treatment that the availability of methadone simply complicates the heroin user's already difficult situation, and that it is better to assist them to relinquish their dependence on opiates in one single, steady thrust. In other areas, however, clinics will prescribe methadone on a longer term basis as a 'maintenance' drug, sometimes although not always with the requirement that the ex-user attends counselling sessions or group meetings.

There are arguments on both sides of this sharply contested professional divide. Methadone maintenance can give drug users somewhat mixed messages about appropriate drug choices, in that the doctor's prescription in effect condones addiction. The police will also sometimes complain that where methadone is available, this brings an added complication into the local heroin economy, because some people receiving prescriptions will be tempted to sell quantities of the drug thus swelling the proportions of the illicit trade in opiates. Nevertheless, many heroin users do find that methadone enables them not only to stop using heroin, but also to straighten out their lives and to discontinue undesirable patterns of behaviour such as thieving or prostitution which had been used in order to support their habits. And as such, it might provide an important stepping-stone towards eventual abstinence. Methadone, viewed in this more positive light, is a means by which the heroin user can 'mark time': standing still, no doubt, in terms of any measurable progression towards abstinence; but at least standing still rather than on some dizzy spiral of crime, prostitution and drug misuse.

Even when heroin users try to break themselves free from this spiral of events, and to 'come off' heroin, they are often ill-prepared for the difficulties that they will encounter – not only the question of getting through the process of withdrawal, which is usually not nearly as prolonged or agonizing as the experience of Linda and Brian, but also the difficulties of securing adequate help. Indeed, the tragedy of Linda's and

Brian's experience was that their agonies were fashioned within their inability to secure what they could recognize as effective help. Once this was forthcoming, in the shape of methadone, they found the transition relatively effortless:

Brian It took a while, like. You have to get used to it, for it to get into yer system, but . . .

Linda But you know it's there. Do you know what I mean? You're not always fretting, 'Where are we going to get us heroin from?' You can try and sort things out, kind of thing . . .

Brian Yeh, I mean it's from doctors . . . not dealers, like. Doctors aren't same as dealers are they? You're not always thinking, 'Is he going to be there?' or owt like that.

Linda It's just . . . you can start to sort your head out wi' methadone, cos there's lots o' psychological things, you know, not just with heroin, but wi't needle and all that.

Brian That's it. Like, methadone sorts out physical side, sort of thing. But it doesn't help to straighten out your head . . . you have to do that yersen.

Linda And that's what we're doing now, like'

One of the arguments against prescribing methadone on a maintenance basis, of course, is that it opens the way to all those subterfuges and self-deceptions by which people persuade themselves that they are doing something to reduce their drug intake when in fact they are doing nothing of the sort. The very same, well-practised self-deceptions by which they might have said that they were 'coming off' heroin, while still enjoying 'a little toot' which 'won't do me any harm'.

We saw in some detail how Cheryl and her family struggled with the problem of her methadone intake, which had at first been excessive, while also struggling with the question of how to define her status. Was she 'off drugs', or not? There was some evidence that she was making a fitful effort to reduce her intake, but it required the constant vigilance of her friends and family:

Cheryl   . . .at first, when I started getting it I were having it to get wiped out off it. Cos if you have enough . . . you can get an hit off it like . . . Phhh, I looked terrible didn't I? Well, I were gouched.

Wendy   She only uses what she should do now.

Wayne   If she uses too much, we can tell straight away that . . .

Wendy   We *tell* her and all, don't we?

Wayne   Aye we tell her. But like, we can't really . . . we can't go on at her, you know what I mean. Because, like, she's got past stage o' using heroin hasn't she? And like she *is* helping hersen now. And I don't take it as same, you know tekking . . . medical stuff like linctus, or owt like that. I don't think it's same as heroin like.

(Cheryl, Wayne and Wendy, early 20s, South Yorkshire)

An alternative medical approach is to prescribe methadone only as an adjunct to withdrawal, whereby the person's dosage is progressively reduced according to a strict timetable over a period of a few weeks, until he or she is no longer physically dependent on the drug. For some people it works and they are able to 'come off' heroin without any of the distressing symptoms associated with 'cold turkey' withdrawal. But it can also lead to that recurring cycle of abstinence and relapse, because although a methadone-reduction course solves the problem of 'coming off' it does nothing to address the more difficult accomplishment of 'staying off'. In some areas, in order to meet this eventuality, a flexible medical policy has been adopted whereby if someone fails to benefit from a reduction course they will be offered a maintenance prescription. Elsewhere, methadone maintenance is simply not on offer and the only option is a reduction course.

Julie is someone who embarked on a methadone-reduction course and subsequently relapsed, and we can usefully trace what this meant to her because there was to be no back-up of a maintenance prescription. Julie had been smoking heroin for nearly two years when she decided to go to a psychiatric unit as an in-patient for a four-week reduction course, having

supported her habit through prostitution for something like
twelve months at this time. The trigger for this decision was
that her boyfriend, who was also a user, had been caught for
shoplifting and was facing a Court appearance. It is a fairly
typical route by which someone discovers the motivation to
'come off', although Julie also had her own reasons, and they
decided to try together:

> 'He'd never been in trouble before . . . anyway he got
> caught for thieving, you know he wanted his own money
> sort of thing. He didn't want to live on me. He doesn't like
> to think that I'm keeping him . . . But we both decided that
> we wanted to come off it, because it was becoming a
> miserable existence really. It was. I was having to go out to
> work on the streets to get money every day . . . now he was
> in trouble with the police . . . We just both decided we
> wanted to come off.' (Julie, 29 years, West Yorkshire)

So far so good. Even better when Julie found that the in-patient
treatment agreed with her:

> 'It was alright, it was sort of three meals a day. I mean, I was
> allowed to go back to bed after breakfast and things like that.
> And they started me off on 30 mills of methadone a day, for
> the first three days. Then it went down to 25 for a few days,
> then 20 until, you know, they were bringing me down to
> about . . . well, when it got to 3 mills a day I said I didn't
> want any more.'
> 'Were you getting any withdrawal symptoms? Did it
> work?'
> 'No it worked. The methadone was great, it was, you
> know I just felt . . . I felt alright. The first week I was really
> tired. And I could go out if I wanted to, you know into town
> or whatever. And I did one Sunday, I came into town . . . I
> went to see a friend and the first thing that they did was
> offer me a hit, and I had a hit. Just one little chase, you
> know, and felt really sick with myself that I'd gone sort of
> two weeks and not had anything. And, you know that was
> the only, literally all I had, that one chase during the four
> weeks that I was in . . .'

It was a bad omen. When she came out of hospital, she quickly slipped back into her old haunts. At first she had no more than the occasional 'chase' now and again with friends, but it did not take long before her habit had built up again to its former strength. Her boyfriend, however, had the Courts to think about and managed to stay off heroin. Julie, increasingly disillusioned by her lifestyle, had returned to prostitution which she had first taken up after her last failed attempt to secure help to 'come off'. Now she could no longer even justify her activity as a prostitute to herself as something which was necessary to support two habits (her boyfriend's as well as her own), and it was at this point that her drug involvement took a further twist on a downward spiral. Finding that the amount of money that she had to earn in order to maintain her habit was becoming an increasing burden, she took the decision to start injecting heroin instead of smoking it, which meant that her daily requirements came down from a gram per day to only one-quarter of a gram. At first, this dramatically reduced the amount of time that she had to spend on the streets, but then the local price of heroin rocketed, so that she was almost back where she started. But not quite. Julie now estimates that she spends at least £30 a day on her habit, injecting most of it but also 'chasing' a little, and she sees no possibility of becoming drug-free in the immediate future. What she would like, she says, is a prescription for methadone maintenance in order to bring some stability into her life. But this is not on offer. In the meantime, Julie and heroin have arrived at a somewhat joyless stalemate:

'I mean, what hope is there, you know? I just accept it now, just do as best I can to sort of support my habit. But what I want really, I want to get a prescription. I know that methadone's as addictive as heroin. But the thing with heroin is that you spend . . . your life revolves round about it, and you spend all day chasing it, you know looking for it, trying to find it, worrying you're going to be able to get some, you know dreading the fact that you're going to wake up and there's not going to be any, you know and the day's just going to be unbearable. I mean there are periods when sometimes, a couple of days when the town's dry and there isn't any to be had, so you're coming down. And you know it's just . . . I just feel that if I had a substitute, I wouldn't bother taking heroin. Because I don't get off on it now, I don't get high on it. I do get an initial rush when I inject it, but then I just feel normal. It just makes me straight, it just makes me normal like anybody else. Because without it I'm . . . just got no energy, aches and pains, horrible sweats, running eyes, nose, horrible taste like being sick . . . you know it's just . . . I feel that if I had a prescription for methadone then, or physeptone or whatever it is, then I'd be able to get my life back into some kind of order . . .'

One might think of people such as Julie in her awful predicament, or Linda and Brian during their own ordeal, as under-labourers within the vast systems of professional expertise, international conferences and academic journals where the question of methadone maintenance is debated and counter-debated with learned precision and the instruments of scientific analysis. What seems to be lacking, as so often in these scientific–technical debates, is any attention to what might simply be a humane response to such difficulties. It would be easy, no doubt, to lecture Julie on the fact that her injuries are self-inflicted; to remind her of her own responsibilities in this sad affair; to tell her that she over-estimates the problems of withdrawal from heroin, and that all she needs to anticipate are a few sleepless nights; or even to inform her that methadone is pharmacologically more damaging than heroin, and that if she were to be given a maintenance prescription then she would eventually find it far more difficult to relinquish than heroin itself. All these arguments carry their own forms of conviction. Nevertheless, when faced with the awful mess of these people's lives, if methadone can enable people sometimes to stabilize their lifestyles, might it not be that all the various arguments and counter-arguments about the advisability of methadone-maintenance programmes become a mere irrelevance, if not even inhumane? This, I think, is what the under-labourers would say to us.

They might be wrong, of course, just as it would be hard to

deny that they have not been wrong on many counts before in their drug encounters. Julie may simply be indulging in yet another form of subterfuge, placing the responsibility for her continuation with heroin on someone else's shoulders, by blaming it now on the fact that she cannot secure a methadone prescription. It could be that in Linda and Brian's case, their daily dosage of methadone linctus has simply lulled them into a passive acquiescence to just another form of addiction. It is not, however, that methadone has made life suddenly easy for Linda and Brian; far from it. They are still living an impoverished, marginalized lifestyle, just as they are still a long way from being drug-free. For Linda and Brian, however, the experience of methadone is that it has enabled them to 'get their heads together', to take stock and address their future. That seems to be not an inconsiderable achievement, given where they have come from. Julie, as things stand, does not even have that option.

Linda and Brian placed great store by what they called their 'spiritual' life, which had been dulled and blunted during their struggle with heroin addiction. But methadone has given them room to breathe again, so that what they had feared might have been lost is now returning. For other people, who were also marking time on methadone, the emphasis was different. Methadone, maybe, was something which enabled them to stop thieving:

'Well, I'm on methadone now like, so I'm sound. I've got on better with my girl, cos she hated the smack like. And with my mam . . . and I won't be going back to Court again. Like, half the maintenance is to stop you robbing as well, you know what I mean. You don't have to go out and buy a bag and that like, cos it keeps you . . . keeps yer straight and that . . . don't go robbing, so you don't go to Court. Like I'm finished with the Courts now, I've just got a fine to worry about like. Then that's it . . . pay my mam all the fucking money I owe her and that like . . . and that's it.'

'What, you're saying that methadone's reduced your criminal activity?'

'Yeh, deffo. You don't need to rob if you've got the

methadone. You just take it, and that's it . . . It's better cos it's pure, and it's synthetic, it's better like. You do get the side effects . . . constipated and that, it gives you the same . . . the itchy nose, and you feel . . . like sitting in the doldrums, if you like, and all that. You do get side effects, constipation . . . terrible that, I've nearly cried before today with that, on the toilet . . . But like, I'd rather have that methadone than buying shit! And running around robbing, and screwing up my ma's life, and all of that like.' (Eddie, 21 years, Merseyside)

For others, methadone offered some kind of emotional security. So that, whereas Linda and Brian thought that methadone only 'sorts out the physical side' and leaves you with the job of 'straightening out' your own head, for Sharon it was precisely the 'mental' comforts of methadone which she valued:

'But, I don't know like. It's security, I think. You know, like when you're on smack or methadone, you feel secure. You can cope with the stress and that like. But when you've got nothing . . . it's the stress I think that really gets on top of you, it's the mental part of it, not the physical I think . . . You know when you're withdrawing, it's the mental part that really gets on top of you, I feel like throwing myself out of the window, I do. But like, them adverts and that like . . . the way they say, "At least I'm still alive" and things, and sitting there all screwed up . . . I don't think anyone's that bad like. I've never seen anyone that bad. But, er, I suppose they've got to exaggerate it a bit like haven't they? Are they proper heroin addicts them?

'No, I don't think so.'

'Hm, I thought so . . . [laughs] . . . I thought there was no way they could be really. I can tell a smackhead anywhere, and no-one's that far gone.' (Sharon, 21 years, Merseyside)

It is notable that Sharon, for whom the initial attraction of heroin was that it gave her a 'buzz' and made her feel as if she were 'walking on air', now gives quite a different account of why she feels that she needs to continue with methadone: it

provides her with emotional security. Her boyfriend is still a
daily heroin user, and Sharon freely admits that she is a long
way from being drug-free. Even so, when asked can she
envisage a drug-free life, at first she hesitates and appears not
to understand:

'What . . . do you mean off heroin?'
'Yes, and no methadone or . . .'
'Just nothing?'
'Yes. Just going to the pub again, maybe . . .'
'Oh . . . that seems miles away.'
'Does it?'
'Oh dear . . . No, well, I think what I'm going to say is,
like, not this week . . . But what I'd like to do is, sort of stick
to methadone all this week . . . and then next week, I'm
going to pick up my script again, and like detox myself. Not
tell the clinic, like, cos if you tell them anything like that . . .
as soon as you tell them, they just cut your script out. So I'm
just going to try and detox myself on the methadone. And if
I can do it, like all well and good, and I can get my fella off
then . . . like, giving him what I don't need . . . That's what
I'm going to try and do.'

It is a pipe-dream, no doubt, with the odds heavily stacked
against her, in that she clearly depends upon methadone at the
moment for dealing with the stresses and strains of her life.
But at least Sharon can now afford to dream again, instead of
just thinking about where the next 'bag' will come from. It
must also seem something of a pity that the inflexibility of the
available services is such that she feels that she must keep her
dreams and her schemes hidden from those very people who
might otherwise be able to help her. This encourages a
secretiveness which lends itself to those very self-deceptions –
especially strong when she has a 'fella' who is still using heroin
– that 'one little toot won't do me any harm'. The loyalties of
friendship which cause her to think of how, within her limited
resources, she can help her boyfriend to come off heroin are
the same loyalties which might also drag her back down again.

In spite of all the hardships that people have experienced
with heroin, they still often harbour residual feelings of loyalty

both to fellow-users and to the drug itself. It is something which once more gives the lie to the self-dramatized tale of the ex-addict that there is nothing but sorrow in heroin. Because there is also pleasure, and sometimes ex-users will try to plot out a future which involves an occasional indulgence which will give them the pleasure without the sorrow:

> 'When you've been off it for a while, you know, it doesn't take much to get a real hit. I'd rather like, if I could . . . what I'd like to do now, is take one every now and then, when I get my giro, about every two weeks . . . Just get a £5 bag, and get really wrecked. And that'd be it . . .' (Kevin, 21 years, Merseyside)

People will sometimes claim that they have arrived at a successful compromise whereby they remain virtually abstinent, with just an occasional encounter with heroin:

> 'I get really jealous of these young users who are new on it. You know, cos when they're first starting they get out of their crusts with a £5 bag. With me, it'd take fifty quid to get like that, even though I've not had a habit since Christmas. Getting that nod is what it's all about, you know what I mean . . . but that's the cruel joke with smack, like, once you're really on it, you don't get it. Like, if you're just using smack to get straight, I reckon you're better off with methadone cos it lasts longer . . . Anyway, I've kicked all that in the head. What I just do now is have a dig now and again, you know, like when I'm pissed off and have the money.' (Gerry, 32 years, Manchester)

These are risky games to play, however, better left as no more than a brief moment of fantasy, to be quickly supplanted by the more enduring possibilities of a future built around something other than the occasional hit:

> 'I used to love the smack . . . Just like me now, if I had a quarter, I'd just put it on a tinny now and *blast* it! But, like, I don't want to, cos I've got my methadone, and I'm happy with that, that sorts me right out. Plus there's no shit in that methadone.'

'Can you see a future without methadone?'

'Everyone at some time, they're gonna come off the methadone . . . I mean, maybe when I'm like . . . I'm going after a place now with my girfriend, my own place to live and that, and . . . eventually have kids and that like. And I think that'll sort me out, you know what I mean? Cos I won't be interested in nothing else . . . just want my bird to be happy and that like. So eventually some day, you're gonna come off it, like. But it takes time, you know, cos for two and a half years all you've been interested in is getting a bag, getting a bag like . . . and you you get used to that. That's a routine for you like. So . . .' (Eddie, 21 years, Merseyside)

Staying off: 'Your life revolves round about it'

This has been a long chapter, because the process of 'coming off' heroin can be a long process. But whether or not someone approaches the question of 'coming off' gradually, with or without methadone, or as a swift self-administered withdrawal, they will eventually face the problem of 'staying off'. And repeatedly, this is said by heroin users to be much more difficult to accomplish. It would be wrong to think of this difficulty, however, as arising from heroin's awesome addictive powers. It is more a question of the way in which, in order to support a heroin habit, people must structure their lives around the effort to secure a continuous supply. As Eddie described it, heroin use was a 'routine' – and a most exacting routine – so that staying off heroin (or methadone) seems to be as much about rebuilding new routines, new motivations and new friendships as it is about avoiding the temptations of the drug itself.

This, of course, is easier said than done. We have already encountered people who managed to 'come off' heroin through a variety of methods, only to slide back into their old ways. Colin, for example, who took himself off to the Isle of Man and seemed to thrive without heroin for six weeks – until he had to return to Liverpool for a court appearance on a possession charge when he was placed on bail on the condition that he lived at his mother's house, whereupon he soon found himself back in the company of old friends and went back on heroin. Paul, who had withdrawn himself on a number of occasions and who was the most eloquent spokesman for the view that 'coming off' was not terribly difficult, but who nevertheless had always found that he slipped back into the heroin scene eventually. Sharon, who successfully completed a methadone reduction programme but then began having a little 'toot' with her boyfriend to keep him company, until she was eventually given a maintenance prescription. Julie, who was back to using heroin again daily within a matter of weeks from finishing a reduction course, and for whom there was to be no methadone maintenance. And then there was Joey, who had been packed off to gaol for a six month period of enforced abstinence, but wanted heroin immediately that he came out:

'Stupid. Like, the first day I got out, it just seemed as if I was turkeying again, and all that. I really did. And I really wanted it . . . I was . . . I really wanted it that first day. Anyway, I got some off a lad. Took it, and I said to myself, "Oh it's only one go." And like, took it nearly every day until Saturday . . . no Friday, the last Friday just gone. I wanted to get off it. So on Friday I took only £2.50's worth; Saturday £2.50's worth; Sunday none; and last night I took a chase off somebody . . . about a quid's worth that's all. So I'm doing alright now, and I'm not turkeying or nothing so I reckon I'm alright. I'm staying off it.' (Joey, 20 years, Merseyside)

Joey did not really believe that last remark himself. He was not that stupid. However, while 'stupidity' might sometimes be self-admitted as part of the recurrent cycle of abstinence and relapse, it was only part. The lure of friendship, of course, is a major influence.

'The last time I was off it, I was doing okay. No problems. But, like, I was just hanging around with nothing to do. And the thing with when you come off is the time goes so slow. It's funny, but when you're on smack, the time seems to fly . . . you know what I mean? And I was just farting about, doing nothing. So I started going down where the mates were, like, not for the smack or anything. Just for a chat and all that, see how they were doing. But they all went dead weird on me, "piss off" and that like; "What are you doing round here, haven't you got no home to go to?" All that. Like, if I wasn't on the smack, they didn't want to know me. Maybe they thought I was gonna grass 'em up, I don't know. Anyway, like I say, I said, "Here you are, then, here's a fiver, who's got a bag?" Just have a toot, you know, show 'em I meant no harm. Well that was it . . . I was on the smack in no time.' (Barry, 22 years, Manchester)

The problem of what to do with time weighs heavily on the mind of the ex-user who has become accustomed to heroin's metronome logic:

'You get up, you've gotta go out, get your money, get your smack, come back, use it . . . You're alright for ten minutes. Go back out again, get money . . . You're turkeying after a couple of hours, can't get nothin', whatever, back out again . . .' (Colin, 23 years, Manchester)

It would be far too simple to describe the release from this rigorous timetable as 'boredom':

'It just seems like the hardest thing in the world to stay off smack . . . Like I say, I've been off it a week, more than a week, but you just go back on it cos it's round here, you know . . . I think, like, unemployment and that has got a lot to do with it . . . with nothing to do, I'm sitting here, like, doing nothing . . . I'm not trying to blame anyone else like, but I'm bound to start thinking of smack again. And I'll probably feel down and all that like. And I'll probably go out and get smack. But like I'm determined this time, I've gotta get off it, because it's fucked up my life completely . . .'
   'What kinds of things can you do to help then?'
   'That's what I'm trying to do, like, do at the moment. Graham [probation officer] he's helping me a bit like, he's trying to talk me into getting a job. But then there's no fucking jobs round 'ere, are there? But, no, be fair, Graham's alright and he's, like, trying to make me get up off my arse

and do something. But at the moment, I don't really know from now on like, I don't know what's gonna happen. I want a job, like, I want to try and *live* . . . It's gonna be hard like.' (Jack, 22 years, Merseyside)

We have met many subterfuges before, through which people justify to themselves why they must stay on heroin; but it would be wrong to think of Jack's reference unemployment as merely another of these ploys. Unemployment might not 'cause' heroin misuse, in the sense of there being a direct one-to-one causal relationship, but we have seen how the absence of effective life commitments such as employment status can hasten someone's passage through the 'grey area' of experimentation into regular daily use. Living with unemployment does, moreover, undoubtedly make it more difficult for people to 'stay off' heroin because of their inability to replace heroin's rigid daily timetable with any other form of meaningful time-structure – as Jack in his own way recognized.

Paul was another young man who acknowledged the problem of how to manage time as one of the difficulties to be encountered when trying to stay off heroin. Indeed, Paul's account was a particularly rich and insightful contribution to our understanding of what these difficulties are about. In his view, as we have already seen, the experience of withdrawal was vastly over-played by the dramatic imagery of 'cold turkey'. The real problem, as he saw it, was 'not coming off, it's the actual staying off that's the hardest thing'. First he described what withdrawal might amount to in his experience:

'As I say, you're not really . . . your first four days are pretty bad, you know, you get the flu symptoms, you sweat and you can't sleep . . . But then after that, the four days, five days, you're on the up then. After a week, ten days . . . you just feel clean in yourself. You know what I mean, you feel the benefit sort of thing. But that's where your will-power comes into it. You know, you keep thinking to yourself, "By this time next week I'll be laughing", sort of thing. That's where a lot of people don't . . . er, after they've done it for two days, they haven't slept, they feel bad . . . before you know it, they're up and out, they want some smack to get rid of it. But if you've got strong will-power, well if you just stick at it, you *can* come off it. As I say, a lot of it's . . . a lot of it's in the head. Y'know, you hear all these people talking about "cold turkey" and all this, well it's not that much.' (Paul, 24 years, Merseyside)

Even so, although Paul took the view that it was not too difficult to 'come off' – and as well as will-power, he acknowledged the help of his family who had actively encouraged him to stick it out, as well as tolerating his bad behaviour in the early stages of withdrawal – he was under no illusions concerning the difficulties of 'staying off'. First there was the problem of changing your daily routines and avoiding contact with the heroin scene:

'Getting out of that little rut you've been in for the last, y'know, twelve months or sixteen months or whatever . . . You know, getting up in the morning, going down for your gear, or getting up and finding some money to get your gear . . . smoking the gear, what have you . . . It's just the actual boredom, y'know, sitting in the house. Like, when I do come off, I just stay in the house. If anyone knocks I tell my mam to tell them I've gone to my sister's – just hibernate sort of thing. It's just getting through the day, just sitting in the house. I know if I go out I'll either meet someone round the area, cos everyone I know is on heroin . . . anyone who'll bother with you. There's still mates who are not on heroin, but because I've been on heroin, y'know, we've drifted apart. So anyone I go and meet is on heroin, and before I know it I'm back smoking it again myself . . . So I just stay in and become a fucking hermit and that.'

On the one hand, the daily routines of a heroin habit can be seen as a dismal compulsion from which the user cannot escape. But at the same time, they had offered to people meaningful structures around which to organize their lives in an eventful and challenging way – 'getting a bag, getting a bag' as Eddie put it – and how to relinquish and supplant these routines is a major problem. Paul's remedy of 'staying off' by staying indoors, thereby avoiding the possibility of meeting heroin-using friends in the neighbourhood, is obviously an extremely limited solution to the problem which could not be sustained for very long. But even in the short term, we can see how it might be limited in its usefulness, if not even counter-productive. Because this passive existence mirrors directly what had been so often found to be unacceptable about the heroin lifestyle – that once you had hustled for and scored your 'gear', all that you were interested in was sitting at home, 'gouching out' in front of the television. Indeed, Paul used exactly the same expression – 'hibernating' – to describe both his solution to 'staying off' and also what he had not liked about being on heroin:

> 'Before I was on it, I used to love going for a bevvy and going to clubs and what have you. But when you get on that, you just don't socialize at all. You just sort of hibernate . . . You get yer gear . . . just smoke yer gear and stay in . . . just don't bother.'

Paul's solution, then, tended to reproduce the very lifestyle from which he was trying to escape, and as such must be deeply flawed. But then, in an area of mass unemployment, what else was there to do? Paul entertained vague ideas about 'getting involved with things, voluntary work, that sort of thing, talking to addicts and helping them through your experiences.' But he also understood that there was something in the contrasts between being on heroin and being off it which made it particularly difficult to 'stay off'. Being on heroin, Paul said, meant that 'all my worries that I had just seemed to float away':

> 'As I say, you just become dead to the world . . . It's just a totally different experience . . . You've got no feelings for anyone . . . and I mean anyone, you know what I mean. Alright, there's times when you sit back and think, "Oh I'm going to get off this gear, then I won't be doing this wrong, and I won't be hurting my mam", but deep down there's something . . . It's not until you're actually off the gear, and you've been off the gear a couple of weeks, that you realize. And you know, it really knocks you sick what you've been doing.'

It was at this point, after getting through withdrawal, when the painful realization of what he had been doing to himself and to other people began to crowd in on him, that Paul found the strain most difficult to bear. Heroin, as he described it, was 'an emotional drug' and this was what made 'staying off' most difficult:

'. . . It really knocks you sick what you've been doing. It's an emotional drug, you know what I mean. It is a very emotional drug. Y'know, when you''ve been off the gear for a week or something, you're in the house with your family and all that, and you realize what you've done in the past, y'know, to get money and that . . . tricked them, lied and stole and all that – well it upsets you, like.'

Later, Paul returned to the same theme:

'You have to . . . sort of start your life again, put a lot behind you. There's a lot of things, like, that I've done that'll always be on my conscience. You know, like bad things I've done, tricks I've played, who I've stole off, and who I've lied to, and who I've hurt. And like, they'll be on my mind, psychological, for a long time. So it's not just the effect of going through your withdrawal and coming off the gear . . . that, to be honest, is a piece of piss . . . You've got to get over the emotional strains and things like that, y'know, things that you try and forget about. But no matter how hard you try to forget them, they're still here. You know what I mean? You've still done them. And there's no way you can make up for some of the things that you've done. Unless, as I say, people forgive and forget.'

And one way that you could forget, as Paul's own experience of the cycle of abstinence and relapse had shown, was to go back on heroin. It made all your worries 'just float away'.

Before he first encountered heroin, and in common with so many of the new heroin users, Paul had enjoyed an entirely conventional lifestyle and had been starting a life for himself. He had a girlfriend, and they had recently had a baby. They were saving to get a place of their own, and almost unusually for young people in his part of the country, Paul had a job.

They had been living together in another area of the city, away from way Paul had grown up, for nearly four years with her mother. Life was not always easy, in fact it was sometimes a bit of a strain, and Paul and his girlfriend had just had a row as young couples do. He had gone back to stay at his own mother's house, intending to stay for maybe a week, in order to let things simmer down. When he met up with his old friends, he found that even after four years things had not changed all that much, except in one important respect: they were just getting into a new drug which had recently appeared in the neighbourhood. A friend of a friend had tried it, and said it was okay. They had all tried it and found it was okay. Paul tried it:

> 'And as I say I took some heroin, and all my worries that I had just seemed to float away . . . Like at the time, when I broke up with my girl, I suppose I could've come home for a week and then gone back and fixed it all up. But it wasn't like that . . . before I knew it I wasn't thinking about my girl or the baby . . . I just wasn't. When I had heroin, I didn't have a problem. I didn't have any worries.'

Now, where was all that? And what does it mean when Paul says that you must 'start your life again'? Faced with Paul's complex emotional reactions to his predicament, one line of thinking would suggest that he might benefit from some kind of therapy or counselling in order to assist him with the difficult business of 'staying off'. Various forms of 'therapeutic' intervention have been devised in the drugs field, embracing a spectrum of treatment philosophies, and often involving lengthy stays in rehabilitation centres or therapeutic communities where the aim is to help people to 'restructure' their lives. But for many of the new heroin users these are not real options. Long-term residential therapy is a scarce resource, for example, and it can also be an expensive commodity. Where people have family responsibilities, moreover, and in particular for single parents, residential facilities are simply irrelevant.

An added difficulty is that so many of these therapeutic programmes are fashioned around what are essentially middle class assumptions. So that, even where only a temporary stay in a residential facility is suggested to one of the new working class heroin users, this can involve sets of standards and values to which they are quite unaccustomed, and which might even seem strange and alien:

> 'Like I don't know anyone, well not yet I don't, that's got off it and stayed off it. I've known them who've stayed off it a couple of months and then gone back on it again. Like, at the clinic, they say why don't I go away to this place, Windy Ridge, and get off it proper like . . .'
>
> 'Where's that?'
>
> 'I don't know where it is. It's called Windy Ridge . . . Like, I knew a lad that went there once to get off it.'
>
> 'Oh, is that the psychiatric unit?'
>
> 'It's like a big nut house, and it's where all the really loopy people go, you know . . . nuts people. And like in the clinic, they offer you like . . . "Do you want to go in there?" Yeh, it's like a psychiatric unit, but you don't get no treatment. You don't get no methadone or nothing. You just go in there to do your turkey. But like, who wants to go to Windy Ridge hospital just for a couple of months with a few freaks . . . And they keep asking me, every time I go there, do you want to go in, do you want to go in . . . you know, working on me. I'd be worse than when I went in . . . [laughs] . . . sitting in rocking chairs! I says, "Thanks, but I'm not into knitting scarves yet" . . .' (Sharon, 21 years, Merseyside)

Various kinds of suspicion and hostility to different forms of psychiatric treatment and therapy enjoy a wide currency within heroin using circles:

> 'Mind you, the trouble round here is you can't get hold of methadone to get off, unless you go in there [the hospital] for group therapy and all that bollocks . . . Honest, last time I was in there I went in with a drug problem and came out with all sorts of problems! . . . Some of the weird ideas they come out with. It beats me what they're on about.' (Gerry, 32 years, Manchester)

This suspicion can even reach such extremes as to suggest to people that what is involved in these kinds of therapy verges

on the bizarre, as if it were voodoo or witchcraft that was being
practised:

Brian There were this fella, Johnny . . . like, best mate at
one time; he went to this Phoenix House didn't he?
And like, he did twelve month in there . . .

Linda But everyone says, 'Oh, I've seen him and he's right
weird.' And he is, isn't he? He's like somebody
else . . .

Brian He's not John. He's not like the old person before he
got on henry, he's different totally . . . it's like a
brainwashing . . .

Linda . . . take that one out and put somebody else in, like.

Brian Yeh . . . they brainwash you, they must do. We heard
that they were saying, like, the reason why you're
into heroin and you're sticking needles in yersen is
because you love your mother.

Linda And Johnny hated his mother, never got on with her.

Brian He did, aye, we knew that.

Linda You know, I mean . . . [roars with laughter] . . . he's
never liked his mother, has he?

Brian Like, that to me were just . . . a load of crap.

Linda They could easily brainwash you can't they? They can
easily put things in your head.

Brian Dead easy to make you believe . . . when you're an
addict, you want . . . you'll do anything to get off it,
and you'll believe anything to get off it, you know
what I mean. They can tell yer owt . . . shit's green,
like, and you'll believe it.

(Linda and Brian, mid-20s, South Yorkshire)

Making a clean break in one's life, of course, need not
necessarily mean entering a lengthy form of treatment.
Sometimes, heroin users who are struggling to 'come off' and
'stay off' in a neighbourhood in which heroin is easily available
will toy with the idea that they should take themselves off to
another area, and remove themselves from the risk of slipping
back into their old habits with their old friends. But where
would they go? And what would they do? It is not just that
these young people often have neither transportable job skills,

nor the resources to take themselves away and to set themselves up in a new area. There are other important ties of kinship and neighbourhood which constrain their choices.

Linda We'd rather do it on us own, in't house like cos . . .
Brian We don't want to leave here.
Linda I mean, where would we go?
Brian There's nowhere else. Like, we belong here . . . this is our town, you know what I mean?

Just as their problems of heroin use originated among friends and in familiar surroundings, so where loyalties such as these are powerful guiding influences in people's lives the question of 'staying off' must be approached in the same terms. It simply makes no sense to see the struggle to break free from heroin as a restructuring of one's life that implies pulling up one's roots and 'starting afresh' – because to run away from these roots is to run away from life itself. Heroin for these young people was not an alien intrusion which burst in upon what was otherwise familiar in their lives. On the contrary, it was born out of that very familiarity, and it must be contested on the same familiar grounds. What then perhaps needs to be said is that the only way to beat heroin is to do it on its own terms, and to learn to live with the fact of its ready availability. This is the way Eddie saw it:

'Like, you've got all sorts of obstacles to staying off it and all that like, going through your turkey . . . but the hardest one's staying away from it like . . .'
'What, you mean knowing it's there?'
'Yeh, it's just like buying twenty ciggies isn't it, round here, you buy a bag like twenty ciggies . . . Like, every-where you go you're bound to bump into someone that you know who's into it . . .'
'Have you ever thought of going to the local hospital where they do a methadone-reduction course?'
'I wouldn't go there. I don't want to go anywhere to get off it. I'd rather stay around the area and get off it. Cos, like, you're gonna have to live in the area aren't yer? So you might as well do it where yer are like.'

'So Phoenix House wouldn't suit you?'

'No. I've got to do it off my own. Stay round where yer are and get off it. If you can't do that, like, stay in the area and beat it, you're never gonna get off it . . .'

'What's the answer then?'

'Like I say, to get off it you've gotta stay in the area where it is, to beat it y'know what I mean? Like, if you go away go gaol you're gonna come out and the first thing you do is go and buy a bag . . . I've seen loads do that. Like, if you're gonna get off it, you've just gotta have your head together and get off it in the same area. And if you can beat that, you're sound, you're laughing. It's not getting off it that's the hard part, it's staying off it . . .' (Eddie, 21 years, Merseyside)

If Eddie is right, and there seems to be so much good sense in what he has to say, then our response to the new heroin users should not be to whisk them away into 'treatment', but to devise forms of help that are accessible in their immediate neighbourhoods. Because that is where the problem originated, and that it where it must be combatted. Although this carries with it one further vital and necessary recognition: so many of the areas worst affected by problems of epidemic heroin use are working class communities which were already battered by a variety of difficulties and deprivations including widespread unemployment and wretched housing, even before heroin began to become freely available. These circumstances, as I have tried to say repeatedly, do not 'cause' the problem of the new heroin useres in any simple-minded sense. But, for people living in these already embattled communities, they do compound the difficulty of 'coming off' and 'staying off' heroin. Because viable lifestyles and identities which can compete with the claims of heroin are not just made up out of emotions and feelings which might be accessible to 'treatment' and 'therapy'. The necessary changes which people must make in their lives also depend on the availability of vital material resources, such as access to decent jobs and housing, around which they can create and sustain viable patterns of recreation, friendship and kinship. In that sense the new heroin problem is not just an individual problem. It is also a collective difficulty, and a collective responsibility, whereby the possibilities for people to lead meaningful and rewarding lives and fashion effective identities in these rundown working-class neighbourhoods of so many of our towns and cities must be rebuilt. It will be a long hill to climb.

Bibliography

Action Committee Against Narcotics (1985) *Hong Kong Narcotics Report 1985*. Government Information Services, Hong Kong.

J. Auld, N. Dorn and N. South (1985) 'Irregular Work, Irregular Pleasures: Heroin in the 1980's, in R. Matthews and J. Young (eds), *Confronting Crime*. Sage.

Beckford, J. A. (1985) *Cult Controversies: the Societal Response to the New Religious Movements*. Tavistock.

Blackwell, J. S. (1983) 'Drifting, Controlling and Overcoming: Opiate Users who Avoid Becoming Chronically Dependent', *Journal of Drug Issues*, 13, no. 2.

Burroughs, W. S. (1977) *Junky*. Penguin.

Chein, I., Gerard, D. L., Lee, R. S. and Rosenfeld, E. (1964) *The Road to H: Narcotics, Delinquency and Social Policy*. Tavistock.

Dorn, N. and South, N. (1985) *Helping Drug Users*. Gower.

Feldman, H. V. (1968) 'Ideological Supports to Becoming and Remaining a Heroin Addict', *Journal of Health and Social Behaviour*, 9.

Henman, A., Lewis, R. and Malyon, T. (1985) *Big Deal: The Politics of the Illicit Drugs Business*. Pluto.

Home Affairs Committee (1985) Misuse of Hard Drugs: Interim Report. HMSO.

Hughes, P. H. (1977) *Behind the Wall of Respect: Community Experiments in Heroin Addiction Control*. Chicago University Press.

Hughes, P. H., Crawford, G. A., Barker, N. W., Schumann, S. and Jaffe, J. H. (1971) 'The Social Structure of a Heroin Copping Community', *American Journal of Psychiatry*, 62, no. 7.

Jahoda, M., Lazarsfeld, P. F. and Zeisel, H. (1972) *Marienthal: The Sociography of an Unemployed Community*. Tavistock.

193

Jahoda, M. (1982) *Employment and Unemployment: A Social-Psychological Analysis*. Cambridge University Press.

Johnson, B. D., Goldstein, P. J., Preble, E., Schmeidler, J., Lipton, D. S., Spunt, B. and Miller, T. (1985) *Taking Care of Business: The Economics of Crime by Heroin Abusers*. Lexington.

Lewis, R., Hartnoll, R., Bryer, S., Daviand, E. and Mitcheson, M. (1985) 'Scoring Smack: The Illicit Heroin Market in London, 1980–1983', *British Journal of Addiction*, 80, 4.

Parker, H. J., Bakx, K. and Newcombe, R. (1986) *Drug Misuse in Wirral: A Study of Eighteen Hundred Problem Drug Users*. University of Liverpool.

Pearson, G., Gilman, M. and McIver, S. (1986) *Young People and Heroin: An Examination of Heroin Use in the North of England. Health Education Council Research Report No 8*. Gower and Health Education Council.

Pearson, G. (1987) 'Heroin and Unemployment', in N. Dorn and N. South eds, *A Land Fit for Heroin: Drugs in Britain in the 1980s*. Macmillan.

Peele, S. (1985) *The Meaning of Addiction: Compulsive Experience and its Interpretation*. Lexington.

Preble, E. and Casey, J. J. (1969) 'Taking Care of Business: The Heroin User's Life on the Street', *International Journal of Addictions*, 4, 1.

Rosenbaum, M. (1981) *Women on Heroin*. Rutgers University Press.

Stimson, G. V. and Oppenheimer, E. (1982) *Heroin Addiction: Treatment and Control in Britain*. Tavistock.

Trebach, A. S. (1982) *The Heroin Solution*. Yale University Press.

Zinberg, N. E. (1984) *Drugs, Set and Setting: The Basis for Controlled Intoxicant Use*. Yale University Press.